The World of André Le Nôtre

PENN STUDIES IN LANDSCAPE ARCHITECTURE

John Dixon Hunt, Series Editor

This series is dedicated to the study and promotion of a wide variety of approaches to landscape architecture, with emphasis on connections between theory and practice. It includes monographs on key topics in history and theory, descriptions of projects by both established and rising designers, translations of major foreign-language texts, anthologies of theoretical and historical writings on classic issues, and critical writing by members of the profession of landscape architecture.

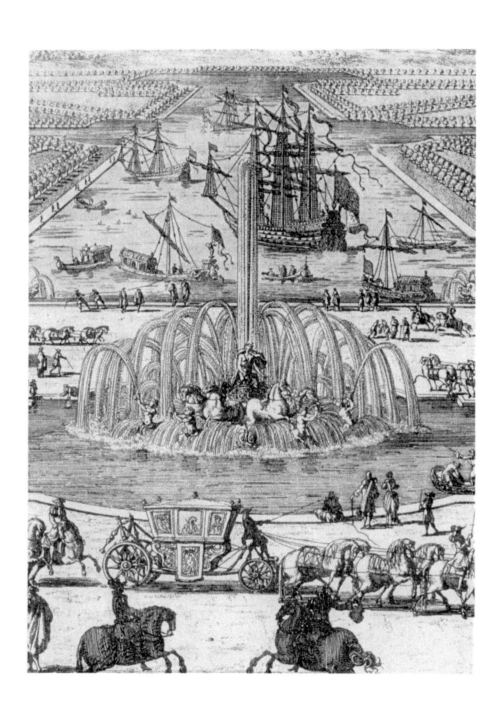

The World of
André Le Nôtre

Thierry Mariage

Translated by GRAHAM LARKIN
Foreword by JOHN DIXON HUNT

PENN

University of Pennsylvania Press

Philadelphia

Publication of this volume was supported by a grant from the
Graham Foundation for Advanced Studies in the Fine Arts

Originally published as *L'univers de Le Nostre*

Published by
University of Pennsylvania Press
Philadelphia, Pennsylvania 19104-4011

Library of Congress Cataloging-in-Publication Data
Mariage, Thierry.
    [Univers de Le Nostre. English]
    The world of André Le Nôtre / Thierry Mariage ; translated by
Graham Larkin with a foreword by John Dixon Hunt.
        p.   cm. — (Penn studies in landscape architecture)
    Includes bibliographical references (p.   ) and index.
        ISBN: 978-0-8122-2136-7
    1. Le Nôtre, André, 1643–1700.   2. Landscape architects—France—
Biography.   3. Gardens, French—History—17th century.   4. Gardens—
France—Design—History—17th century.   I. Title.   II. Series.
SB470.L4M3713   1998
712′.092—dc21   98-35185
                                                                  CIP

Frontispiece: Grand Canal at Versailles (print by Gabriel Pérelle).

Contents

Illustrations

Foreword

John Dixon Hunt

The name of André Le Nôtre (sometimes Le Nostre) is synonymous for many with what is usually called the "French formal garden," a style of landscape architecture indissolubly linked with the social and political culture of Louis XIV and above all the great creation of Versailles. In France, not surprisingly, Le Nôtre is every-where proudly acknowledged and invoked: indeed, to him are attributed, often more hopefully than accurately, any garden design with a suggestion of *parterres de broderie*, straight lines and controlled vistas. If Queen Elizabeth I or George Wash-ington slept here and there, it seems that Le Nôtre laid out gardens everywhere. Furthermore, the gardens that we associate with Le Nôtre are conventionally, not to say tendentiously, contrasted to the "English," picturesque or landscape garden for which Lancelot ("Capability") Brown stands as an opposing avatar. The French are so dedicated, in fact, to Le Nôtre's version of the garden that they have tended to descry any movement into France of its rival English forms.

Le Nôtre's genius is not in dispute. He was a master of spatial adventure, and his designs are a combination of optical mastery and grandiloquent theater. Yet he always exhibited a true feeling for natural materials (earth, trees, water — even sky) at their most expressive. The list of works to which his name can be confidently attached (with or without collaborators) is extensive; they all exhibit both a subtle and confident response to the specific topography of a given site and a masterful deployment of a repertoire of design effects — canals, avenues, allées, parterres, ter-racing, vistas — that have subsequently come to be deemed his trademark.

Given Le Nôtre's prominence both in French garden history and as the de-signer most associated with a particular mode of landscape architecture, the ex-tent and richness of the scholarship and analysis devoted to him are wholly to be expected. A cluster of distinguished French historians — among whom we think immediately of Alfred Marie, Marguerite Charageat, Ernest de Ganay, Pierre de Nolhac — along with a handful of equally accomplished foreigners — F. Hamilton Hazelhurst in the United States, the late Kenneth Woodbridge in England, Gerold Weber in Germany — have provided us with a documentation, analysis and in-terpretation of Le Nôtre's work that few other landscape architects (if any) have elicited.

The general effect of this substantial body of writing has been, in part unintentionally, to establish André Le Nôtre as a towering figure, a unique creative genius, sui generis. Though it is usually acknowledged, to be sure, that in most projects associated with his name he was a collaborator, a team player in the intricate and complex systems of cultural invention and promotion that Louis XIV controlled, Le Nôtre has nonetheless achieved a stature and significance that celebrates his oeuvre above everything else. And in a similar fashion, the style of place-making associated with him has been credited with a distinction and formal difference over any other.

When Thierry Mariage's book on Le Nôtre was published in Belgium in 1990, it did not challenge the stature or genius of this French national garden-maker par excellence. But with a tact that tended to underplay Le Nôtre's considerable achievement, Mariage sought to reposition him in French garden history. If his work comes over as far less radical than it actually was and is, this is due partly to his impressively wide research that so clearly sustained and authorized his fresh perspectives and partly to the minimum of fuss with which he fashioned his case. Graham Larkin's translation happily communicates that rare combination of mastery of materials and modesty of manner.

Mariage's approach employs essentially three strategies. Above all, he contextualizes Le Nôtre. He situates his work at the culmination of long and intricate traditions of land management, many of them fostered by monarchs before Louis XIV. Within the French history of rural property and agronomy, itself depending strongly on new ideas in cartography, hydrology, military engineering, and the state politics of land use, Le Nôtre's work can be seen to assume new significance without losing its distinction; Mariage also explores social and architectural developments in the château and their effects on gardens. Le Nôtre was innovative neither in his mode of exploiting a given site (its genius loci) nor in his invocation of general schemata of the seventeenth-century garden. But if we can stop being distracted by such claims, we may better recognize his contribution in enriching and organizing garden forms and giving them a new and exciting ensemble. In this connection, Mariage deploys his most radical critique of garden history orthodoxy: he refuses to accept that "French" and "English" styles are historically, as stylistically, separate and opposed. Instead, assuming that both are formal expressions — that is to say, forms of representing the natural and cultural world — he can rightly appreciate Le Nôtre's invocation of both modes; nor does this involve him in the teleological fallacy of supposing that the Frenchman is a "Capability" Brown *avant la lettre*.

Penn Studies in Landscape Architecture are therefore proud to make this excellent study available in translation; it can already be said to have influenced analyses of French garden art, so its circulation in English will ensure an even wider impact. We shall continue to translate and publish other foreign language books of distinction in the field; thinking freshly and well about landscape design and its cultural origins and motives needs to observe no frontiers, linguistic or historical.

Introduction

The pleasure garden originated when the organizing principles of subsistence enclosure were reconstituted along aesthetic lines. Its history is that of a separation never fully consummated. Taken alternately as a model of organizing the world and as an encapsulation of an idealized world, this safeguarded, rule-bound, encoded space needed only to have its value system exported. The process was underway in sixteenth-century France, and culminated in the seventeenth century.

The classic garden cannot be reduced to parterre broderies or the forms of bosquets. Its emergence entails certain transformations of the environment based on an exploitation of the existing site and a knowledge of the latest cartographic and geographic techniques of mapping and inventory. Hence the emergence of long avenues and star-shaped crossings, networks of axes engendering new spaces within which the garden acts as epicenter.

The World of André Le Nôtre is a deliberately ambiguous title, meant to evoke the artist's environment as well as his oeuvre. This book does not set out to provide a chronological inventory of his works, a task already admirably achieved by Ernest de Ganay. Nor does it strive for an exhaustive critical analysis, which in any event would not fulfill the pressing need for an examination of Le Nôtre's milieu. Traditional art historical interpretations have only served to secure his place in the Pantheon of scholarly history. Such studies tend to center on specific instances, and on the Vaux affair in particular. By contrast, I have striven to evoke the intriguing image of a man who was more than just a brave, pragmatic, and talented gardener. The period covered corresponds to the length of his life (1613–1700), save for a few excursions that will serve to clarify certain lines of descent and longstanding circumstances. In short, I have found it useful to restore the classic garden not only to its immediate context, but also to its place in extended historical time (*le temps long de l'histoire*), to quote Fernand Braudel.

When entering this domain, we should be wary of formal filiations based on simple morphological comparisons. Elm-lined avenues and canals are not entirely unique to the seventeenth century. Likewise the notion of Italianism, with all its implicit links, scarcely justifies the spate of genetic explanations too readily invoked in this domain. Nor will hastily drawn oppositions to the principles of the English garden stand up to rigorous analysis. Although there is clearly some kind of constructive intention behind both French and English gardens, the distinction between these two means of expressing a cultivated landscape is less clear than we might wish it to be. For instance, both forms borrow decorative motifs from the Orient, and they open onto the world in a similar fashion. One style invites us to set off on canals, expressing the desire for expansion and conquest, whereas the other sums up a world in the process of colonization. Instead of seeing the succession of these two versions of the European garden as a sudden reversal triggered by some fashion—notably Enlightenment anglomania—we should assume that the history of gardens (like the history of ideas) exhibits a certain measure of continuity.

In the form that they have come down to us, seventeenth-century gardens have lost their relationship to the environment, and hence almost all of their significance. A predominantly functionalist interpretation will readily lead to a story of a gradual sterilization of space. It is also a mistake to view these gardens as isolated, intrinsic works of art: they make sense only as part of a larger network, organized over several decades under particular socioeconomic conditions concurrent with the instigation of administrative reforms and the establishment of large infrastructures. Moreover, contrary to general belief, classic gardens are not all of a piece; examination of the plans demonstrates a different solution for each context and a continually shifting arrangement of the various elements.

To maintain some validity, I have limited the field of enquiry to residences belonging to what might be called architecture cultivating royal domination (*l'architecture régnicole*). This became widespread in the Ile-de-France region after Francis I's return from captivity in 1526, and continued throughout the seventeenth century despite economic and political fluctuations.

The copious documentation for this period is too disparate to allow for useful comparisons. Hence we need to rely instead on the campaign of land-use maps, and especially on the more systematic administrative plans, from the second half of the eighteenth century. The list of existing sites is much shorter, since fully intact seventeenth-century parks are rare. Many, such as Villeroy, Chilly, Le Raincy, and Juvisy, have completely disappeared, leaving only the vaguest outlines within a residential fabric. Others, such as the châteaux of La Grange at Yerres and Courson-Monteloup, were redesigned to conform to nineteenth-century English fashions.

In order to assess Le Nôtre's specific contribution, we need to compare his own work with previous or contemporaneous works of a similar nature. The present study relies heavily on the evidence presented by the relatively well-preserved park of Courances and its previously unexploited archives, in addition to Jacques Boyceau de la Baraudière's treatise, which is the only original piece of theory on the subject. I have also drawn comparisons with the structure of the park at Vaux-le-Vicomte. The Vaux connection is less important for causal reasons (such sumptuous residences being common enough among *financiers* of the time) than for the fact that it breaks the previous silence surrounding Le Nôtre's oeuvre. I have chosen to go against the grain of received ideas by asking whether Vaux is indeed an original garden, and if so, why?

By revealing the unsuspected role of various parties coordinated by Le Nôtre, the royal building accounts help us to clarify his duties early in the reign of Louis XIV. Memoirs, works by academicians, inventories, and anecdotes will also enable us to determine how important the great parks were to the enterprise of territorial representation and codification that was beginning at the time. Sometimes a text affords a fleeting yet fascinating glimpse of Le Nôtre the theoretician. These piecemeal additions to the overall results of the analysis can help us appreciate his universality.

Insofar as it supports an order ex nihilo, the park is the beginning of modern spatial relations; it completes the breakup of land parcels and (like our own great feats of civil engineering) it resorts to expropriation. Nor are topography or hydrographic networks spared. Declivities are created in flat terrain, hills are razed, rivers are diverted.

In order to understand these developments we will need to rediscover practical geometry, a discipline linking the layout of gardens with astronomy, cartography, and even the art of fortifications. There are evident parallels in the techniques of geographers and gardeners, whose constant collaboration is documented in period memoirs and accounts.

And so the homogeneous grid used in city projects and garden designs gradually gives way to a type of polarized structure that is flexible and differential, an ancestor of the modern overall plan (plan de masse). Indeed, the classic garden is the seedbed of the urbanistic articulation of space, a connection implicit in theoretical writings as well as administrative documents. Here we find the beginnings of qualitative differentiation among different places and functions on the basis of contiguity, transition, and density. The park — with its codifications, its classifications, and its graduated arrangements of plant types — is in some respects the origin of modern zoning. In extreme cases, it becomes no more than a carefully regulated transitional space extending into the forest, its use determined by the rules that Jean-Baptiste Colbert modified in 1669. This development represents a new level of enforced interference into private property that anticipates the records of modern urbanism. Post–World War II methods of territorial management are really just a reactivation of a concept first launched in the seventeenth century. The process involved political consolidation, economic expansion, the establishment of large-scale infrastructures, the origins of perspectival sightlines, and the beginnings of coherent space management.

Establishment of the Classic Landscape

1

MUTATIONS OF THE SEIGNEURIAL RESIDENCE

The Return to the Land

Stemming from the High German word *gart*, meaning palisade, the word garden designates an enclosed space, an extension of the lodgings dictating its form. The medieval *hortus conclusus* was a secure and fairly secret place that never strayed beyond the walls of the fortress or its immediate vicinity. The late fifteenth-century garden at Amboise was still conceived along these lines.

The classic garden, characterized by its grid layout and its use of open spaces, is not simply the by-product of a fashion in the decorative arts. Its form is bound up with the Renaissance transformations of the seigneurial residence. The return to the land in the late sixteenth century was a response to civil disorder, the impoverishment of the nobility, and the will of the royalty. We can gain a general sense of the history of France in the years surrounding the 1589 accession of Henri IV from the *Histoire du Roi Henry le Grand* written by Hardouin de Péréfixe for the instruction of the young Louis XIV. Hardouin's book describes how the festivals of Henri III compelled the majority of gentlemen to break up the family possessions in order to buy precious metal trappings and equipment. In fact, the crisis of seigneurial revenues and the decline of *droits de justice* dates back to the late Middle Ages. From the time of the Hundred Years War (1339–1453), noble life was generally synonymous with debt. Profits depreciated throughout Europe, where the ruling classes of different countries struggled to achieve the status of landed squires who were both producers and merchants.

In France the flow of ideas initiated by the state-sanctioned arrival of the Protestants led to the diffusion of a developed proto-bourgeois ethic of patrimonial management. Around 1600 the royal entourage developed the idea of the lord as *bon ménager*, a country gentleman living off his own resources or attending personally to the management of his land. Following a king clad in gray fabric without lace or gold, rational landowners needed to be sober: those who wore "their windmills and their aged forests on their backs" were met with scorn.[1]

The ideal of a kingdom suddenly transformed into a "hive of innocent bees ever eager to show off their industry and to gather wax and honey"[2] reserved an important place for the garden, both as the country's organizational base and as a model of territorial management. Today, economic historians recognize that the food garden should be given primary importance, even with respect to labor and cereals, whose fluctuating returns for a long time constituted the scholars' sole argument.

Olivier de Serres is generally considered the precursor of this development. Born in 1539 in the Vivarais, he acquired the Pradel estate around 1558, and with the help of ancient agronomic tracts he forged his own idea of a well-run manor. Indeed, he implemented these ideas thirty years before Henri IV instituted the ideology of national reconstruction, and forty years before the publication of his own writings. Despite the marked success of the nineteen editions of his *Théâtre d'agriculture*, published between 1600 and 1675, he should not be viewed as an isolated visionary. For, as Martine Gorrichon explains in her thesis,[3] the relative prosperity of agriculture in the first half of the sixteenth century, resulting from a long period of domestic peace, awakened the Renaissance interest in working the land. Numerous agronomic tracts were published around 1550. Some, like those by

Figure 1. Axonometric perspective and plan of the château of Bury (late fifteenth century), after Jacques Androuet du Cerceau, showing the abandonment of the foursquare fortress. The *corps de logis* stands out, and the adjoining wing bordering the canal is reduced to a simple gallery on the ground floor.

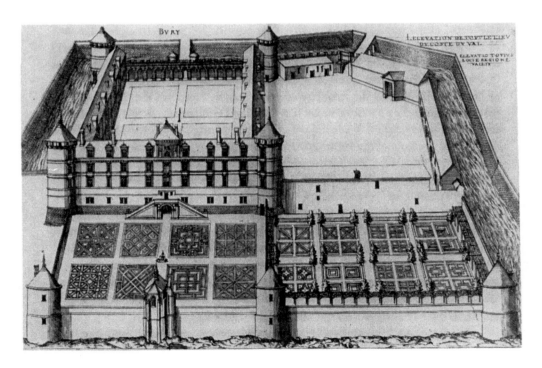

Charles Estienne, Jean Liebault, and Bernard Palissy, were kept in print for more than a hundred years.

The ideal villa was traditionally divided into the *pars urbana* (the living quarters), the *pars rustica* (the farm), and the *pars fructuaria* (the earth). According to Gorrichon, de Serres's originality lay in the intimate linking of farm and living quarters. The plates by Jacques Androuet du Cerceau provide some models of this association (Figure 1), subsequently followed by the majority of country mansions and perhaps even the *hôtels particuliers* of the seventeenth century.[4]

The Split Between the Château and Fortifications: From the Quadrilateral Fortress to the Maison Plate

Whether one considers the internal organization of the residence, the relationship between interior and exterior, or the links to the surrounding territory, it is clear that there were radical transformations in seigneurial living habits between the early sixteenth and mid-seventeenth centuries.

The proliferation of country houses and the modification of the castle type

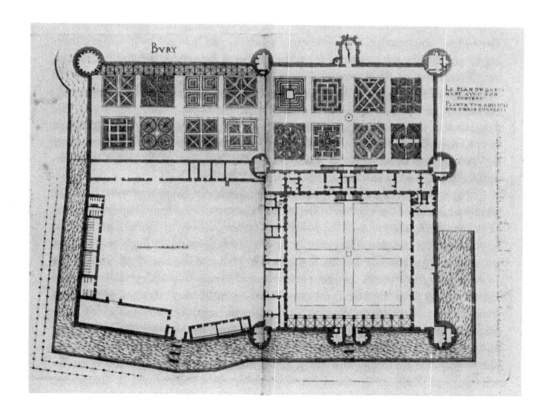

Figure 2. Axonometric perspective and plan of the château of Amboise, from Jacques An-drouet du Cerceau. The later medieval garden is still a space of modest dimensions annexed to or integrated with the building.

began in the second half of the fifteenth century. Defensive elements gradually di-minished, becoming little more than seigneurial symbols. This ultimately rapid evolution can be attributed to various factors: some technical, like the use of artil-lery; some ethnological, like the discovery on the Italian campaigns of a notably more elaborate lifestyle; and some political, like the strengthening of royal power. The ballistic explanation is the one most generally put forward by historians seek-ing to explain the development from the medieval fortress to the classic château. Yet this convenient architectural Darwinism can hardly account for such factors as the loss of feudal power, the extension of national territory and the monarchi-cal system, or the concomitant transfer of defenses to the country's borders. The migration to the frontiers culminated with the network of strongholds designed by the Chevalier de Clerville and then by his successor Sébastien Le Prestre, sieur de Vauban. New urban-scale fortifications eventually replaced the scattering of fa-milial defensive units and the mosaic of *droits de justice*.

The mutation of building types occurred gradually, beginning with the timid transformations of the very early French Renaissance. These were largely confined, as in the well-known case of the château of Lude (Sarthe), to changes in outward appearance; for instance, a bay of superimposed windows might begin to interrupt the continuity of machicolations. But soon the plan and the overall massing began to mutate. In the fifteenth century the château of Plessis-Bourré foreshadowed this movement by lowering one of the wings of the quadrilateral fortress, which until then had been identical on all sides. During the sixteenth century, this access wing was most often transformed into a gallery enlivened by a monumental portal, as at Bury or Verneuil. The final stage of the evolution of this U-shaped structure is a simple physical enclosure, consisting of a perforated wall or grill enabling one to see out, as at Chilly or Grosbois. Likewise, as we see at Blérancourt or Courances, the *corps de logis* breaks away from the entrance pavilions. The latter elements

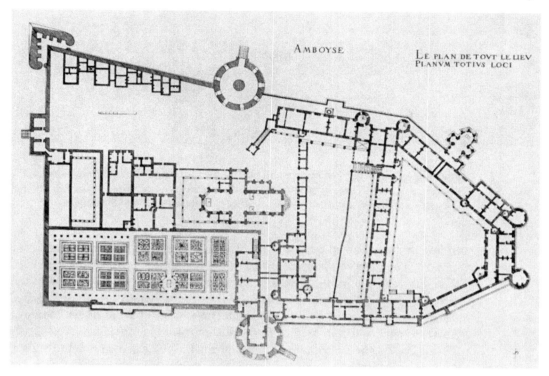

AMBOYSE

LE PLAN DE TOVT LE LIEV
PLANVM TOTIVS LOCI

ultimately disappear, resulting in what we now refer to as Italian-style compact massing, and what the captions of Claude Chastillon's prints refer to as *maisons plates* ("flat houses"). The resulting form is the archetype of the classic residence. It is situated on a slight elevation, vaguely reminiscent of the feudal prominence. While the front of the building still evokes towers and dungeons, it also has its own characteristic features, such as transparency and open spaces.

There were certainly some exceptions to this gradual evolution, since the Château of Madrid built by Francis I was already a *maison plate* and at Challuau there is already a compact form. Cardinal Richelieu's 1628 edict ordering the demolition of fortresses and their transformation into country mansions simply confirmed an evolution that had extended over 150 years.[5] Far from being initiatory in this respect, this decree was mainly directed at fortresses erected or reused in times of civil unrest, and followed on the request made to Henry IV by the Notables assembled in Rouen in 1596.

Emergence of an Axial Relationship
Between the Residence and Its Exterior Space

The counterpart to these transformations in castle architecture was the extension of the garden, beginning around the early sixteenth century. The new openness evident in prints by du Cerceau[6] and clearly manifested in the park at Blois is

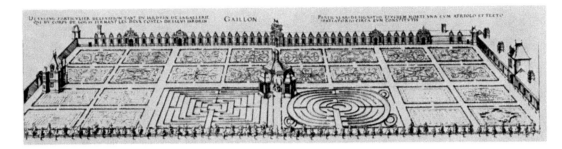

Figure 3. Axonometric perspective and plan of the château of Gaillon, from Jacques Androuet du Cerceau. This early sixteenth-century scheme is characterized by the extension of the garden to the space outside and the absence of an axial relation to the building.

invariably accompanied by some form of enclosure. More important, in the development of new projects rather than extensions or reworkings of existing buildings, there emerged a relation of axiality and concordance in the positioning of the *corps de logis* and the garden, whose main lines converge into a single and unified composition. Examples of this type include the works of Philibert de l'Orme at Anet, Verneuil, and elsewhere. Indeed, thanks to his Roman sojourn (1533–36), de l'Orme has long been credited with introducing Italianate garden styles to France. Although the transmission of forms no longer seems a straightforward matter, we cannot deny that his works reveal a new coherence, and that there might be some relation to the gardens of the Vatican Belvedere and the Villa d'Este at Tivoli.

The Hôtel Particulier *and the Country Mansion*

In addition to the split between château and fortifications evident at Lude and along the banks of the Loire, we can see a development resulting from the newly sedentary nature of the monarchy following the captivity of Francis I—namely, a double residence that is both urban and rural. From this point onward, two types of architecture, the *hôtel particulier* and the country mansion, will emerge concurrently. During the classic period the hôtel and the country mansion exhibit the same formal give-and-take found in apartment layouts and the organization of gardens. And so we find ourselves confronted with a world of similitudes in the Foucauldian sense, with models that interpenetrate and interfere with one another at different levels. These relations, which are both formal and economic, are not specific to the seventeenth century. They can already be observed in ancient Roman villas, where the living quarters are referred to as the *villa urbana* —an obvious reference to urban life.

Since the Middle Ages the term *hôtel* had been used to designate the urban residences of monarchs and *grands seigneurs*. Whether aristocratic or bourgeois, the *hôtel particulier* represents an introverted lifestyle at the center of an urban land

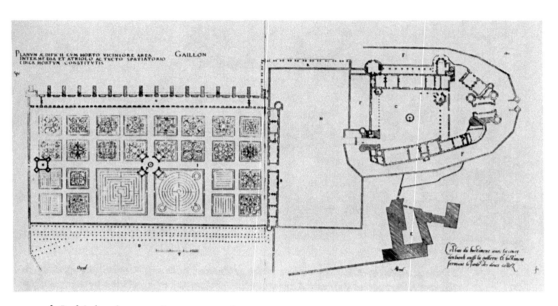

parcel. In his book on early seventeenth-century Parisian architecture Jean-Pierre Babelon elucidates the connection between this image of family self-sufficiency and the model provided by the farmer.[7] The seigneurial architecture of the countryside had a decisive influence on its urban counterpart, at the heart of which we find the forecourt or service court, along with various places for storing provisions.

Country mansions tended to cluster in the Paris region, a pattern reinforced by necessity during the civil strife of the last quarter of the sixteenth century. At this point there emerged an entirely new type of rural economy, in which the *financiers* and bourgeois members of the Parlement played a role that equaled or excelled that of the *grands*. Further on we will examine this colonizing tendency in the suburbs and surrounding countryside during the early seventeenth century, a move that led to the emergence of the great gardens. It is important to emphasize the shift, in the space of barely a century, from a subsistence-level seigneurial habitat, regenerated by the domestic economy following the wars of religion, to the immense lineaments of the classic garden. Such a profound transformation cannot simply be attributed to the *otium* of the ruling classes.

The garden of Villandry, today reconstituted in all its vegetal polychromy, represents an intermediate stage in the shift from the primacy of food to a visual emphasis. Foodstuffs and decoration are here intermingled, yet already the concern with creating a pleasing image is beginning to detract from the necessities of subsistence. This transitional stage is a fundamental link, since from here until the end of the seventeenth century the garden is increasingly extended and abstracted from material contingencies. At the very least we should observe a radical break in which the kitchen garden becomes a separate category that is kept apart from the general layout — a layout that, however abstract, clears the way for full-scale planning.

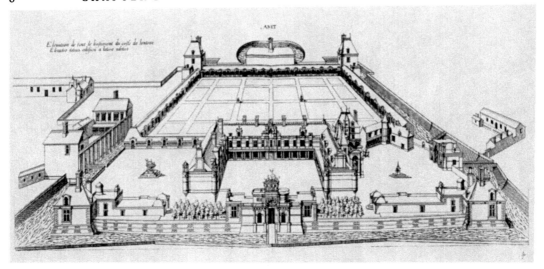

Figure 4. Axonometric perspectives of the gardens of Anet and Verneuil respectively, from Jacques Androuet du Cerceau. After 1550 there emerges an axial relation between the building and the exterior space.

PROTECTIONIST POLICIES AND ECONOMIC PLANNING

Redeployment of Activity

The protectionist policies of Henri IV, which centered on family structure and proper land management, were by no means static in their aims. They served to restructure the foundations of the kingdom in order to increase individual revenues and thereby promote the circulation of goods. The evident desire for planning required the establishment of necessary infrastructures. In his official history of the reign, Hardouin de Péréfixe notes that "from all quarters the king received estimates from anyone able to help make commerce better and easier, to supply commodities to his subjects, to cultivate and fertilize the most unfruitful areas. He wanted, as far as possible, to make rivers navigable; he had bridges and roads rebuilt and the main roads paved."[8]

Seventeenth-century society was fundamentally rural. Even in urban enclosures, gardens, stables, and cowsheds helped impose the solar rhythm of the rural economy. Rather than being havens of uniformity within a highly diversified countryside, cities were content to distinguish themselves by means of a ferocious defense of their administrative autonomy. The great originality of Henri IV's project was its holistic vision of rural space aiming to unite France in a dynamic and productive force. This is the same period which Marc Bloch sees as instigating capitalist methods in agriculture.[9]

The English model is common in writings of this period, especially on the subject of the segregation of the poor: Maximilien de Béthune, duc de Sully makes this

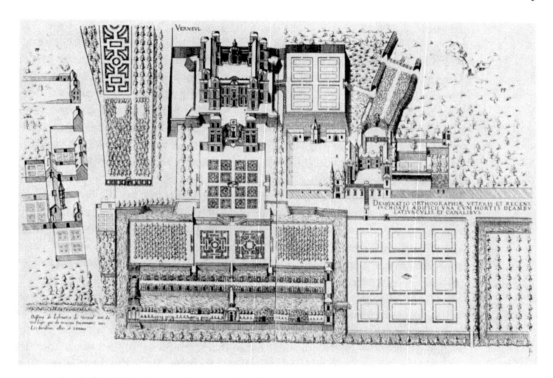

connection in his *Mémoires*, as does Antoine de Montchrestien in his *Economie politique*. Barthélemy de Laffemas (a tailor, a *valet de chambre* of Henri IV, and an influential theoretician whose proposals the king submitted to the Assembly of Notables in Rouen in 1596) envisioned the allocation of manufacturing work throughout the territory. Each diocesan seat would have its own manufacturing office run by important merchants and artisans, and would have at its disposal two houses where beggars of both sexes would be housed and obliged to work. Laffemas even goes so far as to propose a division of labor between cities and small villages: "the former will make silk fabric, the latter wool cloth, and likewise all other merchandise will be ordered in such a way that both of them proceed according to regulations." [10]

This highly structured vision of the country, which will resurface some years later with Antoine de Montchrestien,[11] is the counterpart to an intensified exploitation of land surfaces, as fallow or rugged areas are banished and marshes drained. The surge in ruralism is promoted by concrete measures. A 1595 declaration by Henri IV protects agricultural instruments and livestock from seizure and bans unjust requisition. Another important step forward is the 1601 edict forbidding hunting in areas with wheat crops or vines between the first of May and harvest time.

Royal Residences and Mulberry Cultivation

Royal residences, urban hôtels, and country mansions were indissolubly linked. Together they served to promote a policy of exploitation and planning stemming directly from sumptuary edicts aimed at developing national products, cottage industries, and the use of natural resources. Mulberry cultivation and silk production constituted a pilot project in this domain. The success of these activities served to counter the widespread belief among agriculturists that the plant would not adapt to the French climate. And above all, this production helped to meet the country's needs with the least possible delay.

It was in 1596 that Henri IV first showed an interest in the silk industry by arranging for some mulberry trees to be planted in his garden at the Tuileries. From this moment on, royal and Parisian gardens took on a new importance, acquiring the reputation for experimentation that they have maintained ever since. Colbert took the process a step further by introducing numerous oriental plants to Versailles, brought over on galleys.

In his chapter on silkworm breeding, Olivier de Serres recounts this process of experimentation and his effort at promoting it: "At the beginning of 1599 I had published a special treatise entitled the harvesting of silk and addressed to the members of the Hôtel de Ville of Paris, so that it would incite their populations to pull from the entrails of the earth the silk treasure hidden there, thereby revealing the millions in gold lying stagnant there. With such riches they could finally decorate their city down to the last ornament." This passage reveals how easily de Serres makes the link between agricultural and urban development. Next he determines the sites most appropriate for the endeavor: "Among the fair places in the Parisian countryside I noted Madrid and the Bois de Vincennes, royal houses capable of receiving and sustaining 300,000 mulberry trees." [12]

The king took an interest in the proposition, deciding in 1599 to have white mulberry trees placed in the gardens of all royal residences. He instructed de Serres and the Baron de Colonces, Surintendant Général des Jardins de France, to gather mulberry trees in Provence, Languedoc, and Vivarais and to acclimatize them to residences in the Paris region. Early in 1601, fifteen to twenty thousand plants were shipped and planted at Fontainebleau, the Tuileries, and the park of Madrid. Silkworm-breeding houses were constructed in all these royal residences under the direction of Manfredi Balbani of Lucca, who was charged with bringing over specialists to supervise the plantings. At the château of Madrid the activities included not only worm-breeding, but also silk-throwing and threadmaking. A complete production center was also built at the Tuileries: "And in order to further accelerate and advance the said enterprise and to demonstrate the ease of this manufacture, his Majesty had a great house specially built at the bottom of his garden in the Tuileries at Paris, fitted with everything necessary for the feeding of worms and for the primary uses of the silk." [13]

The royal domain was not the only testing ground. In 1602 60,000 mulberry trees were brought from Languedoc for Parisians to plant in their own gardens. Barthélemy de Laffemas attests to the success of this operation when he notes that "for an example and clear proof, in the garden of the Hôtel de Retz, 18 pounds of silk were produced by the mulberry trees, without any of the worms dying, and sold for 84 écus." [14]

After the success of the Parisian enterprise a decision was made to extend this activity throughout the kingdom. Contracts were drawn up with the four *générali-tés* of Tours, Lyon, Paris, and Orléans for the supply of plants, seeds, and worms. One of the most interesting documents is the one connecting the royal council with the bourgeois Parisians Jean Le Tellier and Hugues Cosnier concerning the promotion of silkworm breeding in Poitou. [15] (The same Hugues Cosnier turns up as adjudicator of the canal works at Briaire, another great planning operation of the period. He even proposes that surplus mulberry trees be used to line the banks of the canal. [16]) Although this expansion project faced stumbling blocks in the form of distribution delays and reticent peasants, it is nonetheless true that the royal and Parisian gardens were at the origin of a great national experience.

Infrastructure Projects

This planning policy also included numerous canal projects that should be viewed as inseparable from the extension of gardens. Further on, in the analysis of compositional elements and themes, we will examine how seventeenth-century canals and gardens merge in a realm of imagery based on fluvial communications. Garden canals are more than simple decor: no less than the celebrated perspectives, they express a desire for open space.

The building of the Briare canal, interrupted by the death of Henri IV and completed around 1642, was just one part of a far more ambitious project. The papers of Sully preserved in the Archives Nationales [17] contain a memorandum from Bradley of August 1604 proposing that the Atlantic Ocean be joined to the Mediterranean by connecting the Rhône, the Loire, and the Seine. The entrepreneurial enthusiasm of this text helps us to understand the importance of the episode in the history of ideas: "from Bourgogne one would be able to travel to Venice in an ocean-going vessel on the Loire and Seine rivers in France, and on the Rhine and Meuse."

Between the eleventh and the thirteenth centuries, the Italian countryside had already been transformed by major drainage, as well as dike and canalization projects. The French effort in public works had been anticipated in the Milan region by the Sforzas. In 1457 the Binasco canal was dug in order to bring the Navilio waters from Milan to Pavia, and in 1464 the Matesana canal was made to bring water from the Adda de Trezzo to Milan. During the same period the Venetian republic was equally preoccupied with the regularization and maintenance of its own rivers. Italian men of science like Leonardo da Vinci made innumerable studies to help advance these operations.

The essential difference between the French and Italian projects lies in the scale and scope of the intention: the government of Henri IV did not limit its ambitions to the linking and improvement of local rivers, or to the doubling of existing basins. The French also expressed the novel ambition of joining different basins by means of canals, and even of linking two seas in an uninterrupted circuit. We can therefore compare two types of juncture. On the one hand, there is the river Garonne, which becomes the Canal du Midi by the end of the seventeenth century. On the other hand, there is the far more ambitious system cutting across the navigation line in the heart of France by joining the rivers in the manner anticipated by Bradley. These two options became the subject of a lengthy debate that ensured an important place for the canal theme throughout the course of the century.

The plotting of routes, avenues, and large garden axes is part of the same general movement. Hence the special importance of the centralization of projects under Henri IV and the creation of the post of Grand Voyer de France (Inspector General of French Roads) in 1599. Over the course of this gradual process of administrative consolidation, Sully marshaled his provincial intermediaries to ensure that he would be at the head of all of the programs and public works. Having purchased the office of the inspector of Paris, the famous minister was also in a position to plan and carry out the great city square projects. In this way, space (both in general and in particular) became a matter of state.

The Inventory of the Country and the Place of Châteaux in the Descriptions

The plotting of canals and roads, and the fact that the proponents of economic nationalism[18] had begun crystallizing their attitudes toward planning, gradually led to a clearer and more global image of territory that transcended provincial particularities (those differences in language and custom that resulted from slow communications).[19] Our knowledge of the administrative geography of ancien régime France is hampered by the lack of uniformity among the governing institutions: the *élection* is a group made up of communities of inhabitants, the diocese a group of parishes, the bailiwick (*baillage*) a group of fiefs. Hence the Paris region (or more precisely the Ile-de-France) is defined in various ways in the seventeenth century, being seen "first as the country in the region of Saint-Denis; second as all of the country enclosed by the Seine, Marne, Oise and Aisne rivers; and third as a great government extending into Picardy, Brie and the Gâtinais."[20]

Travel accounts and descriptions of the provinces are not especially reliable before the seventeenth century. They are often produced by authors who have never visited the places described, and plagiarism is frequently the rule in such works, which tend to concentrate on antiquities, the foundation of settlements, and especially local peculiarities. The *Dessein de la description entière et accomplie du très florissant et très célèbre royaume de France* (*Outline for the complete and thorough description of the flourishing and very famous Kingdom of France*) was published by André du Chesne in 1614 as an offer of service to the regent. Having noticed that France (unlike Italy, England, or the Netherlands) does not possess a reliable description of itself, du Chesne proposes to undertake the necessary travels if he can acquire appropriate financial backing. In his description of "[t]his kingdom that is worth a hundred,"[21] du Chesne evokes not only the episcopal cities that excel in the "sumptuousness of buildings and edifices,"[22] but also "numerous other beautiful *places* and châteaux."[23] His mention of these features is very significant, since from this point on country mansions will become increasingly prominent in the descriptions, at precisely the time when their spatial dominance is becoming more pronounced. One increasingly finds detailed descriptions of such features as the suburbs of Paris, villages, royal and noble residences, and the châteaux of Meudon, Saint-Cloud, Madrid, and Saint-Germain, with particular emphasis on refined decorations, *rocaille* grottos and other Italianate marvels. The sudden emergence of these descriptions (aimed at travelers and *curieux*) predates the first scientific pictorial records of France by at least fifty years.

Over the course of the following decades, the descriptions gradually took on the form of truly useful guidebooks. By this point, travel was deemed a necessary activity for "the nobility and the children of the best families destined for professions and public service; such as those who will serve as councilors in the Parlement, as *maîtres des requêtes*, or perhaps head judges and state councilors. And among the nobility, those who aspire to become local governors, marshals of France, or governors of more distant provinces, so that they may become familiar with these regions, learn about them, and benefit from them."[24]

Greatly influenced by Jesuit teachings, which we will examine below, this invitation to discover new territory corresponds to such developments as the rise of the class of royal officers, the social evolution of the nobility, the growth of public offices, and the consolidation of the state. These changes coincided with the first attempts at graphic inventory during the 1630s. One example is Christophe Tassin's 1639 *Plans et profils de toutes les principales villes et lieux considérables de France* (*Plans and profiles of all the major cities and considerable places of France*). The emergence of cities as entities was therefore more a product of strategy than landscaping.

With the passage of time, descriptions of places and other itineraries placed increasing emphasis on the château. By the eighteenth century the subject came to dominate all others, with most studies devoted to the Paris region. For instance the *Guide fidèle des étrangers dans le royaume de France* (*Faithful guide for foreign travelers in the kingdom of France*), compiled by Alcide de Bonnecase, sieur de Saint-Maurice, and published in 1672, contains "the description of all the cities, châteaux, country mansions and other remarkable places that one might encounter on one's journey." On the other hand, alongside a *Nouvelle description de la France dans laquelle on voit le gouvernement général de ce royaume et la description des villes, maisons royales, châteaux et monuments les plus remarquables* (*New description of France showing the overall government of this kingdom and the description of the most notable cities, royal houses, châteaux and monuments*),[25] Jean-Aymar de Piganiol de la Force published in 1736 a *Description de Paris, de Versailles, de Marly, de Meudon, de Saint-Cloud, de Fontainebleau et de toutes les autres belles maisons et châteaux des environs de Paris* (*Description of Paris, Versailles, Marly, Meudon, Saint-Cloud, Fontainebleau and all the other beautiful mansions and châteaux in the Paris region*) to which he devoted no fewer than eight volumes. During the same period, the campaign of land-use maps, and later of administrative plans, reaffirms the role of châteaux as structures organizing the landscape.

Sadly, visual documentation of the countryside from the seventeenth century is virtually nonexistent; as Marc Bloch has noted, the beautiful seigneurial maps did not become common until the following century.[26] Indeed, despite the work of cartographers like Damien de Templeux, Tassin, and Sanson, there seems to have been little interest in mapping fenced-in expanses of land: people tended instead to rely on lists of places. Moreover, maps made before 1660 are little more than toponymic enumerations, in which typography is more important than indication of relief. Such is the case with the *Carte des environs de Paris à 15 et 20 lieues à la ronde* (*Map of Paris and environs within a radius of 15 or 20 leagues*) written by Thomas Auvray, Sieur de Garel, and published in 1650. Here rivers and ponds appear only as names. Only the maps by the Abbé Delagrive or the Cassini hunting maps make clear the network of country mansions in the Paris region. These documents supplement the evidence provided by the administrative plans since they alone provide a uniform scale for comparisons.

THE REHABILITATION OF THE FRENCH NOBILITY

The Rise of the Class of Royal Officials

The period extending from 1610 to the advent of Louis XIV (and, more symptomatically, to the Vaux affair) was a time of speculative private initiative. Gardens were conceived by and for the great bourgeois dignitaries, representatives of a movement toward land ownership thriving in the Paris region. This development ended when the state resumed its grip on spatial management, regaining power by means of cartographic campaigns and ambitious design projects.

We cannot understand the rapid emergence of country homes without considering the history of rural property. As Père Claude de Varennes notes in his 1639 *Voyage de France*, "aside from the celebrated buildings of Fontainebleau, Saint-Germain-en-Laye and others that serve as temporary royal residences, there are numerous princes, seigneurs and prelates who are delightfully installed in the countryside inside very expensive houses and châteaux." The great bourgeois dignitaries are omitted from this enumeration, and yet it is they who were actually the principal actors in this reconquest of the system of agrarian land ownership.

The merchant bourgeoisie emerged from the wars of religion in a favorable situation, making rapid fortunes through speculation in commodities, shares, and interest-earning loans. But the discovery of America and the Spanish importation of gold led to a crisis in France, whose principal effect was a rise in land prices. The new economic situation gave rise to significant problems, especially for the revenues earned by the nobility whose rental incomes shrank by an average of two thirds. Even the occasional conversion to tenant farming could not stem the tide of family insolvency that permitted the merchant class to acquire both property and titles. Such is the process of mutation that the French nobility underwent at the turn of the seventeenth century, a change aggravated by the loss of their administrative and judicial role, and by the establishment of permanent armies.

The decisive rise of the state, evident throughout the seventeenth century until around 1680, was achieved by means of a steady increase in the number of offices.[27] Access to these administrative posts required expensive juridical knowledge, which, along with accounting, formed the basic knowledge enabling the merchant class to serve the needs of the state.[28] By allowing for the inheritance of administrative posts the 1604 Edict of Paulet further strengthened the position of this group, whose members were mainly descended from three or four generations of ascendant rural families. Most were working farmers made wealthy through improved sowing techniques and loans. The social ascent of the Colberts is a case in point. In a thesis devoted to this family, Jean-Louis Bourgeon shows how the ancestors of the famous minister began in the fifteenth century as laborers and masons before moving successively into merchandising, banking, and finance.

Generally members of the Parlement or royal councilors, such office holders constitute a class that was economically vigorous yet socially reactionary. One might assume that, as *parlementaires*, they would have served as counterweights to royal power, but in fact this was not the case. Their power surfaced only when their own privileges were threatened by such measures as the creation of new offices or special contributions affecting their position. The royal officers who owned country mansions and fiefs in the Paris region were allied to the aristocracy by marriage and were hoping to establish their sons in military careers.

The Colonization Process in the Paris Region: Parks and Agrarian Land Parcels

During the same period, pleasure residences came to impose their geometry on a rural land system that had previously spread in endless confusion. Establishing parks is hardly a simple process, and the massive expropriation of land at Vaux was by no means typical of the first half of the seventeenth century. Land parcels had to be purchased through a gradual process of consolidation and exchange, all of it following procedure and duly notarized. Only then could one attend to the marking out of plots and plantings.

Because the park insinuated itself into the existing land system through a series of conquests, it was integral to the rural countryside, rather than simply being tacked on. It took shape gradually, and its relationship to the surrounding space was not as discordant as it is often made out to be. The result of a regrouping of land *avant la lettre*, it bordered on *champtiers* (woodland areas) and perpetuated within its enclosures the food-producing traditions inherited from the feudal economy. As we shall see, the domain of Courances is a conspicuous example of this situation.

Although the Vaux affair of 1661 marked the end of private initiative in the formation of gardens, art historians should be careful not to exaggerate the importance of this political event. Nicolas Fouquet's fête really signaled the end of a type of neo-feudalism and the dawn of a state dynamic. Henceforth the tone would be set not by wealthy private estates, but rather by great construction projects on a regional or national scale. Indeed, historians may have overestimated the importance of the Vaux park simply because it is one of the few surviving examples of the impertinent luxury that aroused the king's jealousy. Similar luxury had existed at the château of Meudon belonging to the *financier* Abel Servien (a colleague of Fouquet) and the château of Maisons belonging to the chancellor de Longueil, as well as at Le Raincy and Evry-petit-Bourg.

In order to account for this multiplication of country mansions, we need to return to the relationship of the Parisian bourgeoisie to the surrounding countryside. The immediate Paris region [29] was attractive because it offered significant tax exemptions. In reality, the influence of Parisian consumers extended beyond the city's borders; hence the distinctive fate of certain areas, such as the region that is now the Département of Essonne. The outskirts of Paris were once a mosaic of gardens, orchards, fields, and vineyards. This was an area strewn with small residential groupings, punctuated here and there by the country mansions of princes, seigneurs, and above all the bourgeoisie.

From the mid-sixteenth to the mid-seventeenth century, three or four generations of bourgeois dynasties bought farms, consolidated domains, and eventually built châteaux. In 1615 Nicolas de Neufville, duc de Villeroy, took a domain of one thousand hectares composed of ten farms, and raised it to a marquisate through the successive purchase of fiefs and seigneuries. The former château of Villeroy was highly significant both for the building and for the park, traces of which still survive. One can point to many other examples of the establishment of large properties: Richelieu owned Rueil and Limours, whereas Claude de Bullion, his Superintendent of Finance, already owned Bonnelles and Bullion, to which he added Wideville, Maule, and Mareil-sur-Mauldre. Established in Chaville as farm owners, the Le Tellier family became seigneurs of the village, and added to it Villacoublay and Meudon in turn. And so with the families of Phélypeaux at Pontchartrain, Arnauld at Pomponne, Lionne at Bercy and Fresnes, and Lamoignon at Baville and

Courson.[30] This process of land regrouping under the pressure of urban capitals was facilitated by the prevalence of very small scale farms, with plots averaging about five hectares each. This situation made it easy for royal officers to exploit the financial difficulties of the lower peasantry.[31]

The Inventory of Country Mansions in the First Half of the Seventeenth Century

The concentration of pleasure residences belonging to royal officials was great enough for certain authors to recommend touristic itineraries lasting several days. As early as 1639, the royal historiographer Denis II de Godefroy drew up a kind of guidebook to the *Belles maisons et promenades qui se peuvent faire autour de Paris* (*Beautiful houses and promenades that can be made around Paris*).[32] In his *Voyage pittoresque des environs de Paris* (*Picturesque journey in the environs of Paris*) devoted to descriptions of residences found within a radius of fifteen leagues, Dézallier d'Argenville proposes four outings, leaving from the gates of Sainte-Honoré, Saint-Jacques, Saint-Antoine, and Saint-Denis respectively.

These two documents can be supplemented with bibliographic studies of famous architects and regional studies, especially in the Département of Essonne and in the territory of the former Seine-et-Oise. Together these sources have enabled us to establish a list of the residences that certainly existed in the seven decades between the succession of Henri IV (1589) and the Vaux affair (1661). This period saw the emergence of a network of parks before Le Nôtre's career was effectively underway; aside from a few modifications at the Tuileries and Luxembourg, there is no complete work attributed to him before Fouquet's commission. Such domains were not created from scratch, a fact that further complicates the problem of dating. In most cases the fief already existed, and a preexisting building was simply modified. Yet in almost every case the exterior spaces — our present concern — were recast and extended.

List of the Country Mansions Created, and Seigneuries Acquired and Transformed, Between the Succession of Henri IV and the Vaux Affair

1. Bandeville
2. Baville (Lamoignon)
3. Beaurepaire
4. Belesbat (Hurault de l'Hospital)
5. Bercy
6. Berny (Président de Belièvre)
7. Bonnelles
8. Breteuil
9. Bullion (Bullion)

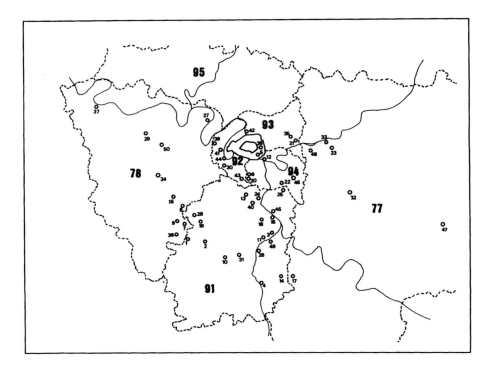

Figure 5. Locations of country mansions. The numbers by the small circles refer to the list of mansions in the text; the boldface numbers are the standard numbers for administrative districts: 77, Seine-et-Marne; 78, Yvelines; 91, Essonne; 92, Hauts-de-Seine; 93, Seine-Saint-Denis; 94, Val-de-Marne; 95, Val-d'Oise.

10. Chamarande (Pierre Mérault)
11. Chantemesle (Hesselin)
12. Charenton (Jean Rougé)
13. Chilly (Maréchal d'Effiat, then Mazarin)
14. Courances (Cosme Clausse, then the Gallard family)
15. Dampierre
16. Evry-petit-Bourg
17. Fleury-en-Bière (Cosme Clausse)
18. Fleury-Mérogis
19. Forges-les-Bains
20. Fresnes (Guénégaud)
21. Gagny
22. Grosbois (Raoul Nouveau)
23. Guermantès (Président de Viole)
24. Juvisy (Michel le Masle des Roches — Antoine Rossignol)
25. La Grange d'Yerres (Duret de Chevry)
26. Limours (Richelieu)

27. Maisons (René de Longueil)
28. Maison-Rouge
29. Maule (Bullion)
30. Meudon (Cardinal Antoine Sauguin — Abel Servien)
31. Mesnilvoisin (Cornuel)
32. Monceaux-en-Brie
33. Pomponne (Arnauld)
34. Pontchartrain (Phélypeaux)
35. Le Raincy (Bordier)
36. Rochefort-en-Yvelines
37. Ronsy (Sully)
38. Reuilly (Nicolas du Plessis Rambouillet)
39. Rueil (Jean de Moysset, Richelieu)
40. Sauvigny-sur-Orge
41. Saint-Cloud (Monseigneur de Gondi, Hervant)
42. Saint-Ouen (Madame de Mauroy)
43. Sceaux (Louis Potier de Gesvres)
44. Sèvres (Moinerot)
45. Soisy-sur-Seine
46. Sucy-en-Brie (J. B. Lambery de Thorigny)
47. Tournan-en-Brie (Tombonneau)
48. Vaudreuil (Girardin)
49. Villeroy (Maréchal de Villeroy)
50. Wideville (Longueil, then Bullion)

Of the fifty country mansions indicated here, nineteen were located in the present Département of Essonne. There are two reasons for this evident preference for the southern plateaus. The first advantage is the quality of the transportation infrastructure, with its roads "pavé du Roy," including the route that the court used to travel from Paris to Fontainebleau.[33] The second advantage is the geomorphology of the region, shot through with fertile valleys and marshes as well as rivers and streams teeming with crayfish — and all within easy reach of the capital. Here we find the food supply for the seventeenth-century Parisian markets; the continuing abundance of watercress beds in our own day is a survival of the old system.

Already during the Renaissance this sector was home to celebrated country retreats such as those of Michel de l'Hospital (Vignay, near Gironville), Ambroise Paré (Ville-du-Bois), and Guillaume Budé (Yerres). The banks of the Seine and the Essonne had long been important sites for building castles. In turn, the gardens of documented residences (some designed by François Mansart) constituted a landscape school by the time of Le Nôtre's early training.

Continuance and Extension of a Fief: The Example of Courances

The notarial acts and succession inventories in the previously unpublished archives of the château of Courances enable us to trace the formation of a classic garden. This new evidence provides insight into the social aspects of landowning and challenges some common assumptions about who conceived these spaces. The first mention of the Courances seigneurie dates to the twelfth century, and the first known feudal seigneur is Jean de Courances, a contemporary of Louis VII. The Courances family died out in the late fourteenth century, when the fief entered into a series of successive sales. Cosme Clausse, minister and subsecretary of state to Henri II, purchased the land around 1550, in addition to Fleury-en-Bière and property at Fontainebleau destined for the construction of an hôtel. The latter structure was built by the master mason Gilles Le Breton, who is known for his work at Fontainebleau, and whose activity at Fleury has been demonstrated by Josiane Sartre.[34]

Courances was inherited by Clausse's second son Pierre, who was secretary of the Chambre des Comptes after 1563. In his day the château was fortified in response to civil unrest, and defended by a garrison of a hundred cavaliers. After becoming the private Conseiller du Roi, Pierre died in 1604. The land passed to his son François Clausse, Grand Maître des Eaux et Forêts for Bourgogne, who fell into debt and sold the lands and seigneuries of Courances and Danemoins to Claude Gallard, Conseiller Notaire et Secrétaire du Roi, on 13 July 1622. Courances remained in the possession of the Gallard family throughout the seventeenth century: Claude Gallard II, Maître des Requêtes Ordinaires du Conseil du Roy, who succeeded his father in 1636 as the head of the domain, died in 1673, ruined by the cost of renovating the place. Claude Gallard III and François Gaillot-Gallard succeeded him, followed in the eighteenth century by the Poitier de Novion and Nicolay families.

Of the documents given some years ago to the archives of the Département of Essonne by the current proprietor of Courances Jean-Louis de Ganay, the most interesting is an important leather-bound 1638 volume enumerating the complete inheritance of Claude, the first of the Gallard family. The first twenty pages of this register contain (along with the conventional notarial glosses) a list of the state of the homesteads that the Sieur Gallard owned in addition to the seigneurie of Courances. Thus we learn that he had a large house in the Faubourg Saint-Germain near the rue du Four—clearly the family hôtel —as well as two more houses in the same quarter, one on the Rue du Cimtière Saint-André and one on the Rue de Bussy; there were also nine other residences throughout the capital. On the periphery, Claude Gallard also possessed a building at Ris and a farm with lands, fields, and woods at Anet-sur-Marne. Such was the land base of the Conseiller Secrétaire du Roi, a model example of the powerful class of royal officials.

This enumeration is followed by a valuation of the buildings of Courances itself, drawn up not by architects but by the master masons Jacques Valissant of

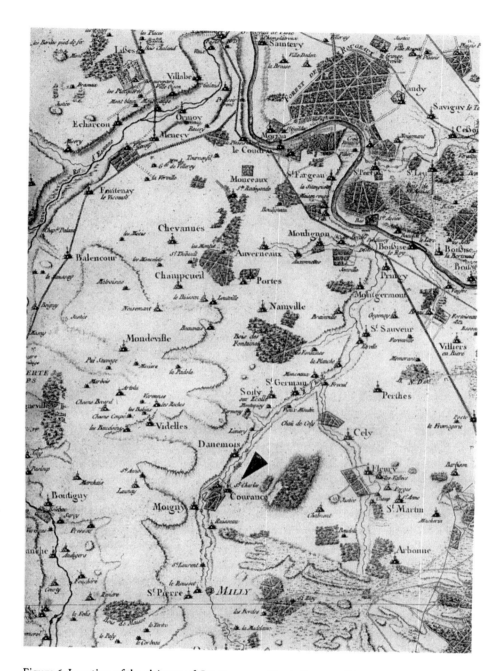

Figure 6. Location of the château of Courances on Cassini's map of France.

Figure 7. Administrative plan of the château of Courances preserved in the archives of the Département of Yvelines.

Fleury and François Couane of Courances. The following description shows how the feudal economy, reactivated by the precepts of Olivier de Serres, was of decisive importance for a site now viewed as an archetype of the classic residence. This description praises "firstly the château of the said place of Courances with the buildings and forecourt of the said château and the structure contained therein," in addition to four barns, a press-house, two wheat mills, and two mills "straddling the river." "Above and beyond this is a mill called the fulling mill, with the forecourt of said château on one side, and the stream of the pond on the other." The placement of these mills is clearly marked on the administrative plan, including one apparently devoted to cloth production, still existing in the present park interior. In turn, the large irregular basin lying to the right of the château, once fed on either side by the river Ecole is none other than the former fishpond, its outlets closed off by hoop nets. This is confirmed by the inventory made at the time of the Revolution, which mentions a small boat with a fishing net moored in a moat. A 1679 notarial document, to which we shall return shortly, provides a more complete description of the château. Here we find a full-fledged country mansion made up of a single *corps de logis*, surrounded by moats enclosing a court, forecourt and flower gardens. I have adjoined this text to the print by Israël Silvestre (Figure 9 below).

It is customary to attribute the transformations of the domain of Courances and the conception of its present appearance to Claude Gallard II, proprietor of the domain from 1636 to 1673, who would have engaged André Le Nôtre for the task. But the 1638 assessment[35] provides us with a description that seriously weakens this hypothesis, challenging all previous efforts at dating the park, as well as the idea of a unitary conception:

Firstly in the Grand Park of the said château of Courances, containing as it presently does by way of enlargements made of the Clos de la Dame, and also of the lands acquired by the deceased Sieur and Dame Gallard and included in the enclosure, which we have valued as follows: with respect to the old park of the said château, in consideration of the willow and alder plantings, full-grown trees, palisades, meadows, a grand canal revetted with sandstone, fountains with hard limestone basins, a spring of running water that makes these fountains work, a water room (*salle d'eau*), fishpond and moats, all of it also revetted with sandstone: a total of 400 *livres* for one *arpent*, which is for the 31 *arpents* and one and one half quarters [i.e. 31⅜ *arpents*], contained in said park before its expansion, following the measurements and surveys that was made in the presence of the said Sieur Gallard by Charon, measurer and surveyor residing at Milly, on 8 April 1627, and delivered to us, two thousand five hundred and fifty *livres*; and with respect to the lands of the former enclosure called the Clos la Dame and other lands acquired by the said deceased Sieur and Dame Gallard for the expansion of said park and included in it, on the basis of 150 *livres* per *arpent*, for the 18 *arpents* and a half dozen quarters by which said park was expanded, 2,793 *livres* 15 sols.

Hence most components of the current park at Courances (Grand Canal, *pièces d'eau*, basins), which also figure in the administrative plan already appear in a 1627 survey as part of the original park, before Claude Gallard's additions. The inventory described in this document thus goes back to before 1622, the year that the domain was sold by François Clausse. André Le Nôtre, born in 1613, was obviously not the author of the project. We must therefore try to formulate an evolutionary conception of the domain, keeping in mind that if Le Nôtre worked there at all, he did so only at a later stage.

Nonetheless we do find an extremely interesting document (near the end of the important volume itemizing the estate of Claude Gallard I, among the acknowledgments of debts) attesting to the existence of business relations between the seigneur of Courances and Jean Le Nôtre, father of André and Jardinier du Roi at the Tuileries. This small paragraph reads:

Item: a thousand *livres* in rent due from master Jean Moriez, attorney (*procureur*) in the Parlement, and Jean Le Nostre, gardener to the king and others, according to the contract concluded before Charles and Corneille, notaries at the said Châtelet [i.e., the Châtelet of Paris, an administrative building], this 18th day of June 1636, amounting in principal to the sum of 18,000 *livres*.

The date of this act is significant, since it corresponds to the end of one phase of expansion. The section of the appraisal cited earlier also informs us of the difference in land value according to variations in plantings, condition, and location. Given the presence of large trees such as willows and alders, along with various costly renovations, the former park is appraised at 400 *livres* per *arpent*. By contrast, the newly acquired lands are appraised at 150 *livres*. The Petit Parc (a term designating the area in front of the château) is valued at 280 *livres* per *arpent* since it contains fruit trees. Some 133 portions of workable land, fields, and vineyards distributed

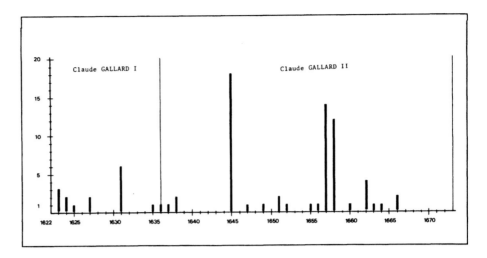

Figure 8. Frequency of notarial acts concerning the transfer of property between the Courances seigneurs and inhabitants of the village, for reasons of park extension, between 1623 and 1660.

throughout the territory, which together comprise the agricultural property of the Courances seigneur, are valued at an average of 60 *livres* per *arpent*. These disparities make clear the lower value of agricultural lands as compared with those enclosed within the park. They also provide a glimpse of the process of regrouping and managing land parcels.

Throughout the archive one finds notarial acts of purchase and exchange relating to the growth of the park. While doubtless incomplete, these documents do help us to determine the phases of expansion at Courances. From the time of Claude Gallard I (d. 1636) we find sixteen acts of property transfer between the seigneur and various wine growers, carpenters, and laborers. Six of these acts were passed between August and October 1631, giving us a general sense of the first phase of work. By the time of Gallard's postmortem inventory in 1638 the park totals 54 *arpents*, or 18.46 hectares (31 for the great park, 18 for the extension, and 6 for the *petit parc*). And in a document of 1679, relating the tribulations of Galliot-Gallard (who purchased the château in conjunction with a creditor of Claude III who was unsatisfied with the bids) the same park measures 190 *arpents*, revealing that it essentially quadrupled in the space of forty-one years.

Under Claude Gallard II, who as we know was ruined by the cost of renovations to the domain, one discovers 63 acts with two surges in acquisition in 1645 and 1657 respectively (Figure 8). Any intervention by André Le Nôtre (which in any case, would not affect the general pattern of the earlier stages) must have occurred some time around these two dates.

In any case, the administrative plan clearly reveals how the park developed between the château and the village by absorbing small manors and *champtiers*.

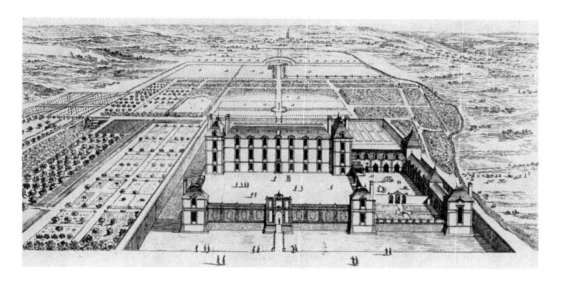

Figure 9. View of Courances by Israël Silvestre. Compare the following description ex-cerpted from a 1679 notarial document preserved in the archives of the Département of Es-sonne. This text corroborates the evidence given above regarding the seigneurial residence:
The château and seigneurial seat of Courances consists of a *corps de logis*, two adjoining pavilions, covered in slate, kitchen, bakery, grain loft above, standing dovecote, gallery and lower chambers at both ends, small flower garden, and three pavilions, of which one is the chapel, the second is the entranceway and drawbridge of the château, and the third consists of a lower chamber and a higher one above with paneling. These three pavilions are covered in slate and the remaining structures such as the dovecote and gallery are covered in tiles, two courtyards, the whole surrounded by broad, flat-bottomed ditches containing running water, with one drawbridge for entering the château and a second for going to the park. By permission of the Houghton Library, Harvard University.

And yet it would be hasty to assume that relations were antagonistic, given the continuity of production within the park and the renewed desire on the part of the Courances seigneurs to provide the village with a basis for development. As early as November 1570, Charles IX granted Pierre Clausse letters patent authorizing his request to set up a market. This authorization, allowing for a market every Tues-day and for two annual fairs, was renewed in 1624 by Louis XIII at Claude Gallard's request.

     As a result of the extension of the château in relation to its rural surround-ings, transverse axes (perspectively secondary yet economically primary) ensured links with the village. Indeed, one can describe the village as woven into the corner of the park, with the point of contact marked by the presence of farm buildings, dependencies that are barely affected by the existing farm of the château. The pres-ence of these structures is confirmed by the same 1679 act that we have cited else-where: "Item: the park adjoining the château both in front and behind, in which are located the food gardens, fountains, canals, fields, young fruit trees, cut wood, workable lands, and allées, at the bottom of the park are buildings serving as a menagerie, covered with thatch and the hen houses with tiles, in addition to a type of forecourt extending to the village, the coach houses, stables, barns, a small house where there was once the fulling-mill, the fulleries, and the canal below."

Our current conception of vast perspectives of impeccably manicured lawns is called into question by the rest of this description, which concerns the areas surrounding the great access avenue "planted with elm trees, beginning at the Garenne de Dannemoins, with a portion of a sainfoin field containing 22 *arpents* stretching from the said avenue on one side and on the other side the river Ecole alongside the château. Item: another portion of workable land comprising 12 *arpents*, stretching from the said avenue on the one side and on the other side the great Lyon road that runs into the avenue."

The Generation of Planners

THE MILIEU AND CORPORATION OF GARDENERS

From Gardener to Landscape Designer: Precursors of André Le Nôtre

Early in the seventeenth century, the gardening profession underwent a transformation identical to the one that had marked the corporation of master masons some fifty years earlier. Although the terminology did not change as it had in the case of architects, the profession acquired a different status while adopting a specialized theoretical knowledge in which agronomy was no longer a key component. André Le Nôtre, who was born in 1613, embodies this profound shift.

Furetière's *Dictionnaire* defines a gardener (*jardinier*) as "one employed in the cultivation of a garden, who sells fruits and flowers. In Paris there is a body, a mastership of gardeners, and gardening regulations." We have seen that in the France of Henri IV, the gardener was the man of the moment, practicing a popular profession in step with political and economic requirements. The prosperity of the kingdom depended on the labor of gardeners, who enjoyed a prestige comparable to that of nineteenth-century engineers or today's information technicians.

We have already examined the particularities of the Paris region (especially the suburbs) during the seventeenth century. Advances in cultivation techniques and planting styles, in combination with sound financial backing, led to the formation of specialized rural professions such as market gardeners and vine growers. At the heart of "that France containing her own India and Peru"[1] lay the Paris region, whose fertility was abundantly celebrated: "the view of Paris is beautiful, skirted by various hillsides and small mountains, streamlets, rivers, fountains, fields, valleys and gardens. There the sky is serene and temperate, and the wheat, wines, waters, wool, hay, fruits, woods and livestock grow with ease and abundance."[2] Before dismissing this flattering description as excessively lyrical, we should note the general agreement among economic historians that the period was genuinely prosperous, with production increasing by 1600 and reaching a peak between 1630 and 1640.[3] And to corroborate André du Chesne's description we have the *Topographia galliae* by Matthaeus Merian, published in 1655. Plates 21 through 29, entitled *Paris wie solche 1620 Anzusehen gewesen*, are a graphic transcription of this countryside; they show suburbs surrounded by gardens looking out onto fields, peripheral villages encircled by enclosures or worked land, and the semirural area just inside the city walls where windmills perch on the bastioned embankments of fortifications.

Four types of people were allowed to sell their homegrown fruits and vegetables at the public markets of Paris: master gardeners, their associates, suburban vendors, and finally the bourgeoisie of the city and its suburbs who wanted to make the most of their garden properties.[4] Around 1600, the community of master gardeners from the city, suburbs, and outskirts of Paris made a series of attempts to obtain royal confirmation of their status in the face of what they saw as unfair competition.[5] They insisted that all candidates for the master status should first complete a four-year apprenticeship under a master of the same profession, followed by two practice years in place of a masterwork. Corporation members also hoped that their children would be able to attain master status "without masterwork or experience, so long as they had been apprenticed, whether under their father or someone else, for the said period of four years."[6] Here we find evidence of the nepotism dear to all trade associations, and which — especially during the seventeenth century — explains the existence of veritable dynasties.

In his *Topographie historique du vieux Paris* Adolphe Berty mentions a 1572 transaction discovered by Le Breton in the archives of the master Trepagne.[7] The transaction was approved by a certain Pierre Le Nostre, a merchant fruit gardener and Paris bourgeois. It concerns the maintenance of six parterres of the Tuileries and was authorized by the Seigneur Derville, a middle-ranking manager of buildings and gardens under Catherine de' Médici. The document reveals the identity and profession of a Le Nôtre who might be the grandfather of the celebrated landscape designer, a connection that has so far lacked definitive confirmation.

The missing piece of this puzzle can be found in Nicolas Delamare's *Traité de la police*.[8] The following text of 16 April 1600 is a request addressed to the king by the corporation of gardeners:

For the preservation of the said trade four jurors will be elected, on the model of jurors in other trades, by the community of the said trade. This jury will make every necessary visit to the said trade, in the city, suburbs and areas surrounding Paris, without requiring permission to visit the said suburbs from the high justices (*haut justiciers*), whatever their privileges and rights might be, since it is a police matter, which pertains solely to the said provost of Paris (*prevôt de Paris*). And below appear various signatures of former young masters of the said trade: Jean le Bouteaux, Benoist Petit, René Jacquelin, La Cruche, Baudoin, Pierre Le Nostre, Jean Le Bref, Pierre Bouton, Bienfait.

The request to reinforce the monopoly of gardeners by extending surveillance rights concludes with the signatures of prominent men in the profession. Crucially, the names include Pierre Le Nostre, in addition to the founder of another dynasty of royal building officers, Jean le Bouteux. Certainly one of the most notable features of this period is the family stability at the heart of the artisanal and artistic trades, and the reinforcement of professional unity through intermarriage. This well-known process of corporate self-perpetuation and protection extends all the way up to the royal administration.

The generation of Jean Le Nôtre, father of André, marked a new departure. As Jardinier Ordinaire of the Tuileries, he was, like his colleagues, essentially required to maintain a portion of the royal gardens. Although the precise status of such men remains unclear, it seems that at least in the early years of their careers they were still partly contractors accountable for the successful completion of the tasks assigned to them, even at the expense of their own fees. This was the case when Jacques Mollet was placed in charge of two new parterres in the Grand Jardin du Roi at Fontainebleau in 1608, where he was to maintain the plantings "which shall remain unharmed or else be replaced with others at his own expense."[9]

The wages of the king's officers enable us to trace the emergence of this social group. Around 1608, alongside Jean Le Nôtre we find Jacques and Claude Mollet, Marc Regnault, Yves and then Simon Bouchard, Jean de la Lande (whose descendants would remain in charge of Saint-Germain), and Jean and Pierre Desgotz (who would be allied through marriage to the Le Nôtre family). As we shall see at Versailles, the division of labor was strictly maintained. In a single park, one person was in charge of the allées and palissades, another of certain parterres or even the orangerie. Only Claude Mollet was employed "for the overall design of his majesty's gardens."[10]

The royal commissions were not especially consistent, and payment was made on the basis of services rendered rather than in a lump sum. So, for instance, in 1624 Jean Le Nôtre received "out of the 300 *livres* that his majesty has granted him for working, whenever necessary, on the design his majesty's parterres and gardens, the sum of 150 *livres*, which is all that he will be paid in the present year for the above-mentioned reasons."[11] Under the circumstances it is hardly surprising that these specialists began to seek private clients.

The appointments rapidly became hereditary: on 25 May 1630, Claude Mollet obtained the right for his son, also named Claude, to succeed him as Jardinier Ordinaire of the Tuileries. The same would apply in turn to Pierre, Charles, and Armand-Claude Mollet. On 26 January 1637, Louis XIII accorded the same succession privilege to André Le Nôtre, son of Jean. The terms of the royal decision were eloquently stated:

In response to the good and laudable report on the person of our dear and beloved André Le Nostre, and in full recognition of his sufficient loyalty, wisdom, and experience in the matter of gardening, expedience and fidelity, for these reasons and others besides, we confer and grant to him by the present [letters] signed by our hand, the Status and charge of Gardener of our Tuileries gardens, which his father Jean Le Nostre currently holds and carries out, who has stepped down in favor of his son on the condition of succession. We delegate [the aforementioned] mandate to the Sieur de Congis, captain of the Tuileries gardens; provided that, after having determined the worthy life and conduct in accordance with the Catholic, apostolic and Roman religion of the said André Le Nostre *fils*, and that after having received the customary oath required in this circumstance, then, on our behalf, he will place in his possession, and deliver to him, the said charge of gardener of our Tuileries gardens.[12]

Here we see the preconditions necessary for the emergence of such a personality and the preponderant role of family circumstances. We should bear in mind the alliances established between the Le Nôtre family and those of other gardeners in the royal household. Jean Le Nôtre, gardener of the Tuileries, had four children:

1. André, who succeeded his father in 1637 and in 1640 married Françoise Langlois. She bore him three children, all of whom died at a young age: Jean-François (1642), Marie-Anne (1658), and Jeanne-Françoise (1661).
2. Elisabeth, who married Pierre Desgotz, gardener of the Tuileries. Their son Claude would become his uncle's disciple and successor.
3. Françoise, who married Simon Bouchard, Tuileries gardener in charge of the orangerie. She bore two daughters, Françoise and Anne, with whom she carried out the job of her deceased husband.
4. Marie, who married the Parisian bourgeois Symphorien Freret. The latter, who only appears in post-inheritance notarial records, did not belong to gardening circles.

Another important alliance was made between Françoise-Andrée Bombes, niece of Françoise Langlois (wife of André Le Nôtre), and Armand-Claude Mollet.

Childhood and Education: The Context of the Grande Galerie of the Louvre

At the age of twenty-four, Le Nôtre was thus considered worthy to succeed his father. Already at twenty-two, in 1635, he was given the title of First Gardener to the king's brother, Gaston, duke of Orléans. At the time the duke lived in the Luxembourg Palace, where the gardens were initially conceived by Jacques Boyceau de la Baraudière, a Protestant gentleman attached to the king's chamber (*chambre du roi*) and the steward (*intendant*) of his gardens. Boyceau was thus the highest-ranking employee at the Tuileries or any park belonging to a royal residence. This stature helps us to appreciate the theoretical import of the treatise[13] published after his death in 1636, as well as the impact of his precepts on the young Le Nôtre.

Childhood was held in low esteem in the seventeenth century. Children had no particular style of dress, hence future magistrates or cavaliers would sport the robes of their profession at a very young age. Swords were granted at the age of ten, and under Louis XIII childhood dueling was not a rare occurence.[14] One usually entered a career around the age of thirteen to fifteen. Contracts for apprenticeships do not mention the age of the candidates, but we can place them at about ten to twelve years of age.

As we have seen, the corporation of gardeners expected a minimum of four years' training. The nature of this training, in keeping with the aspirations of the royal gardening corps at the height of its development, is described by Boyceau de la Baraudière. His educational project immediately reveals the influence of Montaigne:

Now just as we choose for our gardens young trees that are of straight trunk, well-grown, well-supported by roots on all sides and of good descent, so we take a young man of good nature, good-spirited, the son of a good worker, not delicate, thus looking likely to grow physically strong with age, in anticipation of which we teach him to read and write, to make portraits, to draw (since on drawing [*pourtraiture*] depends the knowledge and judgement of beauty and the fundaments of all mechanics); not that I think he must go as far as painting or sculpture, but rather that he attend to those particulars regarding his art, such as compartments, foliage, moresques, arabesques; and the other things that ordinarily make up parterres; as he improves in drawing he should be taught geometry for planning, partitioning, measuring, and aligning; and even, if the boy is gifted in architecture, [he should be taught] architecture so that he has an understanding of the limbs (*intelligence des membres*) required for the construction of forms, and arithmetic for the calculation of the expenses that he will have to deal with. If possible he should learn all of these sciences at a young age, so that when he is old enough to work in the gardens he can begin with a spade to work with the other laborers . . . tracing his designs in the ground, planting and clipping parterres.[15]

This is more properly a program of study than the training of a young apprentice. Practical training and the necessary work experience are supplementary. Evidently the traditional gardening education, in subjects like agronomy, is dispensed with in order to establish a discipline closer to architecture and decoration: a grounding in the graphic arts certainly seems a far cry from horticultural production. In short, we are witnessing the birth of a new professional category, that of the landscape architect. We know that Le Nôtre had a pronounced taste for painting thanks to his apprenticeship in the workshop of Simon Vouet. Less well known is the importance of practical geometry, a far-ranging science encompassing the art of fortifications, surveying, astronomy, and cartography. Further on we will explore this aspect of gardening knowledge in more detail.

In his desire to overhaul the system of corporations and eliminate obstructive red tape, Henri IV favored the establishment of a colony of expert artisans in the Grande Galerie of the Louvre, which became a privileged enclave in the French craft system. Everyone working there was lodged in the Louvre and Tuileries, a stone's throw from the working residence of the Le Nôtre family on the garden grounds. It is within this context of artistic effervescence that Le Nôtre spent his childhood and adolescence. Working alongside the painters, sculptors, printmakers, clock-makers, and tapestry-makers living there were Etienne Flantin, maker of mathematical instruments, and Marin Bourgeois, painter and maker of moving globes. One could also find Jacques Alleaume, the architect, engineer, and professor of mathematics, who is known to have helped conceive fortifications throughout the east of France.[16] It is among such men that we should seek the real masters of André Le Nôtre. Historians have speculated that Le Nôtre might have worked under François Mansart or Louis Le Vau. Yet although Mansart produced a great number of gardens (Maisons, Fresnes, Evry-petit-Bourg), there is no evidence that Le Nôtre spent time in his workshop. On the other hand, we are often reminded that the royal architect Louis Metezeau, was concierge of the Tuileries Palace, and that Louis Le Mercier collaborated at Wideville and Chilly with Simon Vouet and Jean Le Nôtre.[17]

Returning from Italy on royal orders in 1627, Simon Vouet was named First Painter and received on 2 April 1628 a patent from the king granting him lodging in the Grande Galerie of the Louvre.[18] Le Nôtre is known to have studied in his workshop; the date of Vouet's induction enables us to conclude that this was not before the age of fifteen. Vouet, who also shaped the careers of Charles Le Brun, Eustache Le Sueur, Pierre Mignard, and Gabriel Pérelle, secured a reputation as a master in the truest sense of the term. He distinguished himself in his youth by accompanying Monsieur de Harlay on his ambassadorship to the Ottoman sultan: in a single sitting he was able to provide the sovereign with a portrait deemed strikingly accurate. This eastern voyage was good for more than one reason, since it permitted Vouet to observe the layout and decoration of gardens. It is even said that he brought back some drawings of arabesques that later served as models for the young students in his workshop. We know that upon his return to France in 1627 Vouet was employed to supply tapestry designs,[19] a task requiring special facility in the execution of floral motifs and knotwork, and explaining Le Nôtre's own expertise in this area.

Simon Vouet was very close to architects. A 1640 inventory of his goods mentions "40 books on architecture, perspective and other subjects relating to painting."[20] He also worked frequently as an interior decorator, a task involving the students from his workshop. As Dézallier d'Argenville notes, "We have from his hand numerous galleries, ceilings and entire apartments that he painted down to the wainscoting and wood panelling"[21] — not to mention rocaille grottoes like the one at Wideville. Here we seem to have a straightforward explanation for Le Nôtre's training and architectural knowledge.

PRACTICAL GEOMETRY AND MEASURING INSTRUMENTS

Triangulation of Space

Maurice Daumas describes the early seventeenth century as a pivotal moment in the improvement and invention of scientific instruments.[22] In the present context, we should note that the complex geometry of classic gardens can be understood as an appropriation of these instruments for a new use. Clearly marks on the land — whether in the form of new towns or gardens — relate not only to aesthetic theory, but also to the technical possibilities of topography. Without the progress in scientific instruments first developed for mapmaking, gardeners would not have had specialized instruments precise enough to plot on the land the far-reaching avenues, *pattes d'oie*, and star-shaped crossings that require a series of stations, angled reference points, and triangulation.

The idea of establishing maps by forming a sequence of triangles based on distinguishing features of the terrain originated in Flanders and the Netherlands around the mid-sixteenth century. The practice was invented by Gemma Frisius, whose 1566 treatise *De astrolabo mathematico* foresaw the development of a new instrument consisting of a graduated circle enabling one to look from one high point in a city to a second elevation, and thence to a third. On the basis of the angles and a single distance one could then calculate the other distances. The Dutchman John-Pieterszoon Dou used this method to plot his own country in 1612, just as his countryman Snellius used it in 1615 to determine the precise distance between two cities.[23] It was soon discovered that a half circle would suffice; this is how Philippe Danfrie designed his "graphometer" (*graphomètre*) in 1597. This name survives today, and we find this instrument among the illustrations to the treatise by Dézallier d'Argenville[24] — definitive proof, if needed, of its use in gardening. The instrument was further perfected around the mid-seventeenth century, when Pierre Vernier[25] improved the precision of its readings. Soon after, the Abbé Picard fitted it with a telescope of the type attributed to Galileo: further on we will consider the consequences of these developments in optics for the measurement of distances.

The title of Philippe Danfrie's book[26] enumerates all possible applications: thanks to the graphometer, one can "measure every distance between the notable things one can see from the place where it is set up, and survey lands, woods, fields, and make plans of towns and fortresses, geographic maps, and in general all visible measurement." This account suggests an interest in producing a graphic inventory of notable places such as towns and fortresses, recalling the concerns of André du Chesne. For Danfrie, the graphometer involves two devices. The one set up on the land is equipped with a swivel mount and a foot that he calls the observer (*observateur*), a feature not unrelated to the laws of perspective. He calls the second device the recorder (*rapporteur*). The function of the latter element, well known today, is to "record (*rapporter*) on the paper, by means of lines, everything seen through the *observateur*."[27]

This dichotomy is not insignificant: the recopying of space also implicates a second phase, that of its practical application. After all, the recorder could reverse the process by beginning with marks on paper and moving to the terrain. It is no accident that seventeenth-century parks were laid out on a more ambitious scale, or that they displayed convergent axes and star shapes. They are clearly the sites of this great inversion of topographical practices leading to large-scale planning. The royal building accounts for the year 1678 furnish proof of this assertion: under the same heading, a gardener named Thierry is paid for plotting roads in the outskirts of Versailles, and concurrently for mapping the surrounding region.[28]

Topographical knowledge was unevenly distributed at the beginning of the century, at least in the provinces. In the notice to the reader of his 1607 book, Elie Vinet gives an image of a countryside in which surveyors can neither read

nor write, can only count by using chips, and can manipulate only the most rudi-
mentary instruments.[29] The latest instruments were therefore known only to geographers, to mathematicians like the ones residing in the Grande Galerie of the
Louvre, and to a few practitioners. Clearly their use demands a certain number of
scientific prerequisites.

While the numerous writers we have mentioned strove to describe the country, cartographers were busy depicting it. The infatuation with cartography was
already underway by the second half of the sixteenth century. Oronce Finé produced the first reasonably detailed map of France in 1553, followed by Jolivet's in
1560, Guillaume Postel's in 1570, and Maurice Bouguereau's *Théâtre Françoys* in
1594. The main advance of the early seventeenth century was the ability, thanks to
new instruments, to move straight to rendering the terrain on site with the help

Figure 10. Graphometer and recorder (instruments used by cartographers for geodesic tri-
angulations), as depicted in Dézallier d'Argenville, *Théorie et pratique du jardinage* (1747).

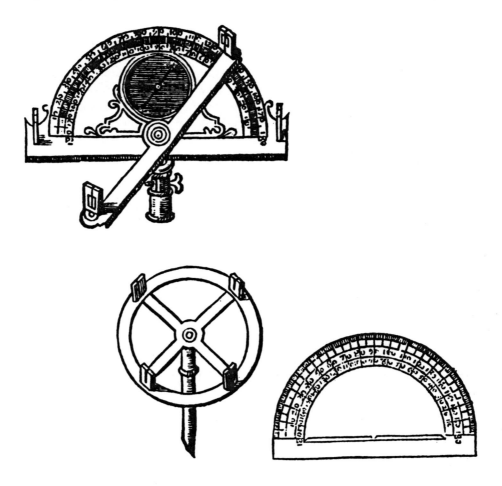

TROISIE'ME PRATIQUE.

*Dresser un terrein entier quelque grand qu'il soit, & le
mettre de niveau.*

La rigole *A B* étant bien dressée, *suivant les deux Prati-*
ques précédentes, le jalon *A* doit être considéré comme im- Fig. III.
mobile, & doit servir plusieurs fois à faire la même opération, pour ache-
ver de dresser en-
tiérement le ter-
rein ; ce qui se
pratique ainsi. On
fiche sur la ligne
A E le jalon, *C*,
à peu près à la mê-
me distance du ja-
lon immobile *A*,
qu'est posé celui
D, dont il ne doit
être éloigné que
de 3 ou 4 pieds
tout au plus. On
pose ensuite la re-
gle & le niveau
sur les jalons *A* &
C, & pour vérifier

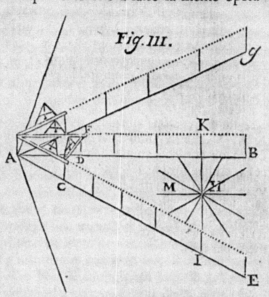

Fig. III.

si cette opération est juste, l'on reporte en travers la regle &
le niveau sur les jalons *C* & *D*, ce qui forme un triangle avec
les deux lignes *A B*, & *A E*, & vous doit persuader de la
justesse des deux nivellemens, s'ils se rapportent à ce troisié-
me. Ensuite *par la premiére Pratique*, vous jalonerez la ligne
A E, & *par la seconde* vous la dresserez bien de niveau, en
y faisant une rigole. Mettez un autre jalon comme en *F*, envi-
ron à la même distance du jalon immobile *A*, que sont posés
les jalons *C* & *D*, & pareillement à 3 pieds du jalon *D*.
Posez-ici le niveau pour dresser la ligne *A G*, en vérifiant la
justesse de l'opération, comme nous venons de dire, c'est-
à-dire, en reportant le niveau sur les jalons *D* & *F*. Dressez

S ij

Figure 11. The triangulation procedure as applied to the leveling of gardens, as depicted in
Dézallier d'Argenville, *Théorie et pratique du jardinage* (1747).

of a portable surveying table. And yet cartographers were initially still more interested in making drawings and fine prints than in producing works with any truly scientific accuracy. They accepted the inexact calculations of Ptolemy without testing or amending them, leading to inaccurate lines of latitude and longitude. These faults mar the work of Jean Leclerc, Damien de Templeux, and Christophe Tassin.[30] Nonetheless, the fact that their maps often indicate distances implies that these men employed the equipment described above.

It is easy to deplore the imprecision of these maps, but such criticism is really beside the point. Instead we should focus on the movement of ideas that led to the increasing commercial success of maps in a period that gave rise to veritable dynasties of cartographers and publishers. The Sanson family dynasty was founded by Nicolas, a Fleming appointed Geography Instructor to Louis XIII, a title that he retained under Louis XIV. The fact that even the monarch found time for instruction in this flourishing discipline is added evidence of its vital place in ideas and attitudes in the first half of the seventeenth century.

Jesuit Education

Knowledge of the physical environment and the means of recording it become a key component of ruling-class education during the first half of the seventeenth century. This education, the prerogative of the Jesuits, produces a veritable generation of planners (*aménageurs*) leading to Colbert and Vauban. The Company of Jesus instituted anthropological studies as early as the sixteenth century. Ignatius Loyola instructed priests sent to distant countries to maintain a frequent written correspondence providing detailed descriptions of local customs and the nature and extent of places visited. While these instructions were clearly intended to hone the methods of propagating the faith, they also constituted an unprecedented documentary record of features like the lay of the land, natural resources, and climate.

The Jesuits understood the needs of the nation and directed their teaching accordingly, emphasizing practical knowledge. The mathematics program in the seventeenth century did not simply cover pure mathematics as we conceive of it today. Applied mathematics was at least as important, if not more so. This consisted of astronomy, optics, perspective, mechanics, surveying, and the art of fortifications. The course taught in 1636–37 by Père Bourdin at the Collège de Clermont in Paris shows us what this teaching entailed:

> The mathematics course is comprised of six principal parts: arithmetic, geometry, music, engineering (*l'ingénieuse*) or mechanics, optics, and cosmography [the former name for geography], which are in turn divided into parts . . . geometry consisting of speculative, practical, resolutive or problem-solving (*résolutive*), measuring (*effective*), relative (*respective*), military, etc.

1. Speculative geometry considers the nature of figures and geometric bodies.
2. Practical geometry deals with all kinds of figures.

3. Problem-solving geometry seeks to determine all the parts of triangles and figures on the basis of parts already known.
4. Measuring geometry, when applied to problem-solving geometry, determines heights, distances, extents — such as the width of a river or a field.
5. Relative geometry makes figures and bodies similar to the ones shown, and in the desired proportion.
6. Military [geometry] concerns fortifications and sieges.[31]

Public exercises in mechanics, optics, and astronomy gave schoolboys the opportunity to display this practical knowledge, while diffusing such knowledge and awakening scientific interest.[32] The instruction was complimented by an apprenticeship in the use of observational instruments; hence classroom walls became covered with maps. Among other developments, a corps of geographical engineers was created in 1624. Called the Engineers for the Fortifications of France and for Camps and Armies, they provided the much-needed topographical documents required for the establishment of roads.

The Arts of Gardens and Fortifications

The arts of gardens and fortifications exhibit similar ways of working the land with regard to the extension of buildings, defensive or otherwise. This might seem paradoxical, since the respective development of these two disciplines marks a division between defensive and domestic aspects of the manor. Yet these two aspects come together on the visual level, which is determined by such features as the line of fire, the "siting angle" well-known to artillerymen, the linking of platforms, and the establishment of declivities, moats, and ditches.

The pleasure residence (with some exceptions like the château of Kerjean in Brittany) essentially loses its defensive character, yet its park borrows a longitudinal profile from the model of fortifications. The work of Mansart and Le Nôtre is distinguished by cuts along the longitudinal axis creating perspectival effects; this division into levels is an application of methods developed for defensive purposes, a link made clear in the illustrations in Jesuit mathematical treatises.

Hence in the case of Vaux, the building commands the clearly detached surroundings, dictating everything from the play of terraces to the interposed canal that must be circumvented, and on down to the sloping esplanade with its ridge.[33] It is likewise significant that in his 1648 *Traité des fortifications* Père Georges Fournier defines the esplanade as "a rising of land that becomes imperceptibly lost in the countryside,"[34] thereby making explicit the analogy with park perspectives.

The comparison cannot be extended further than this borrowed method of organizing large axes using low angles, since the stronghold is isolated, self-enclosed, and self-sufficient, a polygon full of hard edges and sharp angles, laid down on ground that tends to turn to desert. Its margins or borders are modeled so as to create a void inimical to growth. By contrast, the classic park is characterized

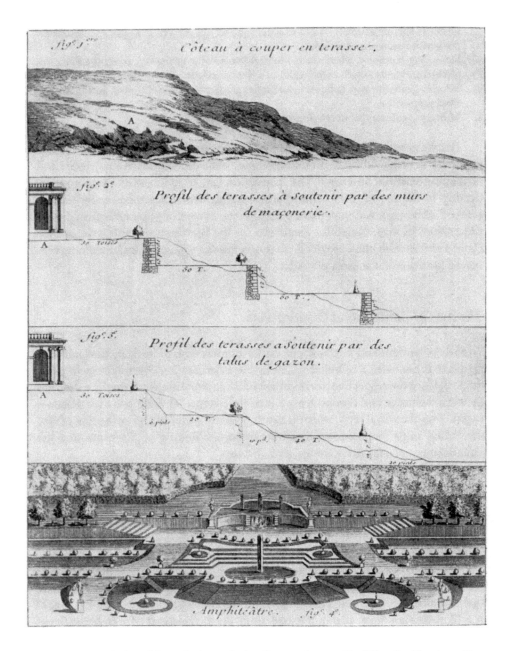

Figure 12. Similarity of the techniques for leveling gardens and building fortifications. Here earthcutting is explained by two plates in Dézallier d'Argenville, *Théorie et pratique du jardinage* (1747) and a figure from Pierre Bourdin, *Cours de mathématiques dédié à la noblesse* (1660).

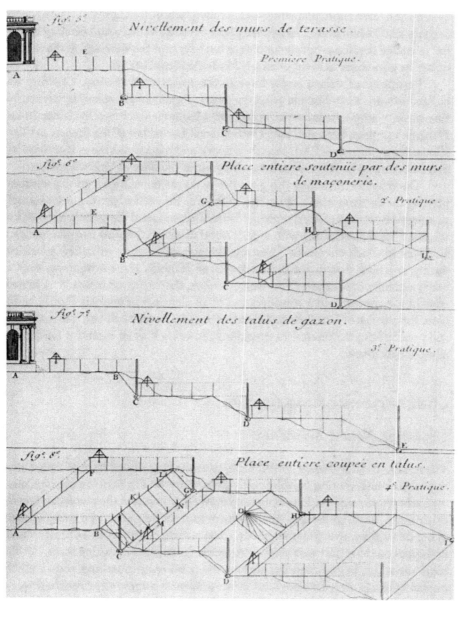

fig. 5. Nivellement des murs de terasse.

Premiere Pratique.

fig. 6. Place entiere soutenüe par des murs
de maçonerie.

2.ᵉ Pratique.

fig. 7. Nivellement des talus de gazon.

3.ᵉ Pratique.

fig. 8. Place entiere coupée en talus.

4.ᵉ Pratique.

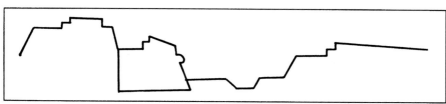

by diffusion, explosion, branching-out, a hub of arborescence; even its boundaries become lost. Le Nôtre even makes use of the dry ditch called a *saut-de-loup* or "ha-ha" to ensure that the property limit does not interrupt the view, and at the château of Issy he goes so far as to suppress any kind of material barrier.

Fortifications were a major issue in the seventeenth century. Le Nôtre was obliged to learn its rudiments using the practical geometry required by his art. We have already noted the influence of Jacques Alleaume. Moreover, his father-in-law François Langlois, Sieur du Hamel, was Official Counciller of the French Artillery (Conseiller ordinaire de l'Artillerie de France), and it is a well-known if curious fact that Le Brun and Le Nôtre were both observers at the siege of Valenciennes.

The art of fortifications also gives rise to the notion of an irregular project exploiting the constraints of a given site. Before the time of Le Nôtre, one had simply proceeded by means of regular geometric models and used the term "orders of fortification" to make the link with architectural canons.[35] But now irregular sites are admitted in which one has to "construct the plan of the place with great precision, noting anything that might cause trouble or furnnish some advantage, such as rivers and hills, old command outworks, towers, châteaux, and moats."[36] A knowledge of the context and a consideration of all elements of analysis should be the basis for any act of development (*aménagement*). As we shall see, garden theory will benefit from the interest in irregular sites, using it as an incentive for the creation of new forms.

CONCEPTIONS OF LANDSCAPE

Landscape, Nature, Agriculture

The notion of natural space, which tends to evoke the original state of a site before any human intervention, enables us to divide the world in two. On the one hand, we find a few isolated pockets of nature scattered throughout the planet, and on the other hand, those landscapes that represent more or less advanced states of managing this nature. Every landscape is a construction, whatever its scale. It initially embodies not only the types of food crops and the method of raising them, but also local variations in common law such as the manner of inheriting and subdividing land parcels. At a different level from family and community organization, the desires of princes or town councilors can lead to the restructuring and improvement of important territories, and sometimes entire regions, as happened in the Po valley during the Quattrocento. But it is above all the eye of the spectator that construes the countryside. Thus considered, it is a section of space, contained within the visual field, to which particular properties are attributed. Landscapes are differentiated by means of comparison, which involves travel; it is significant that *voyage* (travel) and *paysage* (landscape) have a common suffix derived from the Latin *agere*, which means to move ahead, implying both movement and regeneration.

The rural landscape is the stamp that man, in the course of his agricultural activities, leaves on his environment. These considerations result in an appraisal of these forms that is not only technical and economic, but also aesthetic. The concern for a beautiful countryside is already present in Marcus Torentius Varro's *De re rustica* of 37 B.C. Varro is intent on viewing the rural landscape as something that moves beyond utility in order to satisfy the requirements of beauty. He also sees landscapes arranged in this way as having an added value over and above the monetary aspect of estate management.[37] The pleasure garden, in all of its concision, can be viewed as a fundamental instance of this aesthetic apprehension of space.

The Landscape of Painters and Gardeners

In a work devoted to the history of the Italian rural landscape, Emilio Sereni observes that in a given society the interest in representing landscapes develops in relation to projects that transform the natural landscape. Hence the vogue for landscape painting depends on economic growth. This certainly holds true for seventeenth-century France. Parallel to the favorable agricultural situation in the early reign of Henri IV, representations of cultivation enjoyed a new status. The first painted depiction of an open field is Louis Le Nain's *Landscape with Peasants* of 1630 in the National Gallery, Washington. Up until this point, no major painter had deigned to represent the commonplace scene of the vast tracts of land in the Parisian basin and the North.

The birth of this fashion coincides with wall paneling in the Louis XIII style. For instance the Maréchal de la Meilleraye's decoration at the Arsenal consists of numerous small panels, each representing a different landscape.[38] And so the painted landscape is transformed from an accessory genre into a genre in and of itself. The inventory of Simon Vouet's property, made for his 1640 remarriage, registers 120 paintings at his house, including 22 landscapes, one of which is evaluated at 150 *livres*—the same price as a *Virgin and Child*. Considering the importance of religious subjects during the Counter-Reformation, this evidence implies a significant status for representations of nature.

We should also consider a remark made by Roger de Piles in his *Traité du peintre parfait* (*Treatise on the perfect painter*):

If painting is a type of creation, then this is even more subtly revealed in landscape pictures than in other subjects. Generally one finds nature emerging from her chaos, and the elements more disembroiled . . . and insofar as this genre of painting contains and sums up all the others, the painter who practices it must have a universal knowledge of the parts of his art.[39]

This passage indicates that the geometric garden is a composition emerging from an idealized conception of nature, and links it to an elevated taste that for de Piles always implies a use (*usage*) "of natural effects, well-chosen, grand and extraordinary and convincing."[40]

It would be impossible to judge the works of Le Nôtre in relation to those of his immediate predecessors and the cultural tradition of gardens without reference to the then current idea of composition. It consists of two parts, invention and arrangement:

> By inventing (*inventaire*) the painter must find and introduce into his subject the objects most suitable to express and ornament it; and by means of arrangement (*disposition*) he must place them in the most advantageous way possible in order to obtain a great effect from them.[41]

From this we can better understand Le Nôtre's originality, which is less a matter of introducing new elements than of skillfully presenting them, according to rules derived from pictorial practice.

Seventeenth-century painting theory was not concerned with the imitation or transposition of nature, but rather with its correction. Among the manuscripts of the Bibliothèque Nationale there is a dialogue on coloring, issuing from two members of the Academy of Painting,[42] that clarifies this attitude:

> "Nature" retorted Pamphile "is not always good to imitate; a painter must select it according to the rules of his art, and if he does not find that which he seeks, he must correct that which is presented to him . . . an able painter must by no means be a slave to nature."

The same theoretical fragment makes an interesting distinction on the level of method between natural objects and artificial (or painted) objects. This corresponds in turn to the contrast that Poussin established between the outward appearance of things and the way that they are manifested in thought. All of this is important for us in two respects. First, the theory of painting aims at the correction or improvement of nature, an idea in keeping with planning practices. Second, we should notice the way in which artifice is raised to an operative principle. This development is of great importance for gardens, and helps to explain their status as constructed spaces made of plants rectified by geometry.

The idea of correction or improvement is commonplace in seventeenth-century thought. It covers such diverse subjects as the establishment of good grammar (evident in the work of Claude Favre de Vaugelas) and the attitude toward preexisting urban spaces implied in the notion of embellishment that seized the administration of Henri IV, a trend examined by J.-P. Babelon.

The Writers' Landscape

The seventeenth century is characterized by a very particular notion of landscape construction. The classic garden is in fact the privileged site of the inversion of graphic practices: the laws of perspective that had regulated pictorial practice since

Figure 13. Illustration by Abraham Bosse for *Manière universelle de Mr. Desargues* (1648), marking the final stage of the regularization of nature. Here the vegetation is so geometricized that it resembles the cut stone in the foreground. By permission of the Houghton Library, Harvard University.

the Quattrocento are now imposed on the site itself. A garden differs from a painting in that it restores the lateral vision absent in the encounter between the observer and the frontal plane. The garden visitor is not a spectator standing outside of the thing represented: he or she is implicated in the totality of the visual field. Walking through a garden with its succession of fresh perspectives is like walking from the foreground to the background of a painting.

Pleasure gardens have always been spaces of sensation and suggestion. While rehearsing all of the traditional themes, the seventeenth-century garden also introduces new elements. Enchantment is now established not by the paradisiacal density of the enclosed Mediterranean garden, but by the pursuit of what is often a very extensive itinerary. These are gardens of discovery. Here you find the great valley to be scaled, the lake casting back your image, the noise of the waterfall that makes you stop and listen. These are *jardins de voyage* by virtue of their very scale, where the canals with their launching points invite departures into the unknown.

All of the effects are produced through the progression and accommodation of sight. The stability of the whole and the richness of detail are invitations to go deeper into a synchronous realm of interpenetrating viewpoints. Void alternates with solid, and all elements arouse a kinesthetic sense of equilibrium. A symbiosis of body and environment arises from the symmetrical framework and the modeling of the terrain. Since the form of the body has perhaps never been so adequately projected onto nature, it is tempting to link the classic garden with Renaissance ideals and with the anthropomorphic landscapes so highly prized in the curiosity cabinets of Le Nôtre's day.

These cabinets assign a prominent place to optical instruments. Progress in this domain served to reinforce the new way of seeing introduced by perspectival centering. Here we should note the growing interest in the landscape (*paysage*) which Furetière in his dictionary considers synonymous with view (*vue*), and defines as "the look of a country, the territory extending as far as the eye can see." Nor should we forget that Madeleine de Scudéry is invariably taken with the beauty of distances. Hence the general conception of landscape emphasizes the envelope surrounding notable buildings or cities. The captions to Claude Chastillon's engravings include three types of expressions that confirm this notion of framing the object: close landscape (*paysage prochain*), contingent landscape (*paysage contingent*), and surrounding or neighboring landscape (*paysage circonvoisin*). The interest in varied landscapes develops alongside an entire movement of descriptive poetry represented by François de Malherbe, François Maynard, Théophile de Viau, Madeleine de Scudéry, and Claude de Malleville. These authors dedicate stanzas to hours of the day, stretches of countryside, harvests, rock formations, and forests.

The Geographers' Landscape

In the first decades of the seventeenth century, the geography of the theater was heavily indebted to the accounts of navigators and the picaresque novel. One did not hesitate to begin an action in Germany, continue it in Rome, and draw it to a close on the banks of the Nile. The concern for verisimilitude and the imperatives of stage design would soon do away with such fantastical peregrinations. Even so, unity of place did not imply a single location; instead the depictions of several far-flung sites simply gave way to a concentration on the surroundings of one city or region. This interest in regional scale clearly bears some relation to the implementation of topographic methods.

Moreover, there is a new acknowledgment of the particularities of local construction already evident in architectural treaties: "Each province has its manner of building for reasons that cannot be considered general or universally relevant."[43] This development corresponds to early attempts at a pictorial inventory such as Tassin's 1636 *Plans et profils de toutes les principales villes et lieux considérables de France* (*Plans and profiles of all the principal cities and notable places of France*). In this catalog of urban forms, the most common mode of representation is axonometric (or, as it was then called, military) perspective. Distinguished mainly by their contours, cities are presented as objects isolated in an agrarian landscape represented by a graphic sign system, and bearing the outline of land parcels. Curiously, the farther one advances into Tassin's text, the better the rendering of the landscape becomes. Whereas the first prints (such as those of Montreuil-sur-Mer or Amiens) simply give an image of the city as an empty envelope set into an equally deserted landscape, the plates treating Lorraine and Brittany, found farther along in the book, provide more detailed information about the grouping of trees, with each image referring to a different essential characteristic. One can also discern hedges and nurseries, with types of cultivation differentiated by tiny conventionalized signs.

Over the course of a hundred years, the geographers' conception of the landscape changes a great deal. In 1609 André du Chesne is content with a rather materialistic enumeration in which France has "a serene and temperate sky, fertile soil, wheat, wine, cloths, wool, water, wood, and cattle that are easily and abundantly found."[44] Here the goods produced are more important than the soil that supports them, and the lyricism is limited to an enumeration of riches. By contrast, in *Les délices de la France* (*The delights of France*) that François Savinien d'Alquié published in Leyden in 1728, we are carried along by a wanderer's reveries and pictorial visions. The country is now notable not only for its productions, but also for "the beauty of its landscapes" including the "charming sight of so many beautiful rivers, fountains, and streams."[45] This aesthetic apprehension of space is accompanied by perspectival and colored visions: "Let us go out for a moment, and walk a little in the least of our countrysides: let us climb on the slope of a small vineyard and attentively consider the beauty of our valleys . . . look at these fields covered with a gay green, which both delight and please us; notice the flowers scattered across the prairies, the enclosed gardens, allées as far as the eye can see, country mansions and parterres full of all kinds of flowers."[46] Clearly gardens played an important part in the radical change in the perception of landscape.

At the same time, these landscapes were being looked at in a way that had less to do with the painter or the writer than with the statistician and *aménageur*. In his *Méthode générale et facile pour faire le dénombrement des peuples* (*General and simple method for counting people*), Vauban considered the social and economic context. Aiming for the most precise inventory possible, he accounted for the location, land productivity, proportion of fallow land, manufactured products and cattle, all in order to establish comparative tables by parish.[47] With him an image of the town's contour is no longer the central concern. We can already detect stirrings of this attitude in Jesuit education. The 1652 *Science de la géographie* (*Science of geography*) by Père Jean François shows an interest in determining "local ownership"[48] and a definition of place that anticipates Vauban's socioeconomic conceptions: "I would give the following definition of place (*lieu*): it is an immobile expanse which precedes the things placed on it, and is capable of supporting them. . . . I mean it to be an expanse for which the essential feature, difference, and primary notion of place is to contain created beings and their extensions." The countryside is thus reduced to a material envelope having lost all symbolic value.

Theory and Forms of the French Garden 3

Theoretical Writings from the Middle Ages to the Seventeenth Century

When examining the period before the pleasure garden acquired an independent status and theoretical confirmation as a completely separate genre with its own laws, we can trace its formal particularities and evolution only through fictional writings, descriptions, and agronomic treatises. Invasions and the spread of Christian morality led to the transformation of the Western garden, which over time acquired an essentially utilitarian character. Only after the crusades do we see a renewal of garden styles, part of a more general search for new styles of living. The *Romance of the Rose*, completed in 1280, belongs to the tradition of the courtly novel and enables us to glimpse, by way of allegories, the composition of an enclosed medieval garden:

I found myself in a large orchard enclosed within crenellated walls, richly decorated outside with images and paintings . . . the wall was high and square, it served as an enclosure for the orchard in place of hedges . . . when I found myself inside, my delight knew no bounds: I believed I was in an earthly paradise. The place was so enchanting that it seemed supernatural. . . . The orchard formed a regular square, as wide as it was long. . . . There were so many different trees that I would not be able to name them all. Know that they were at a suitable distance from one another, certain among them set apart by a space of more than five or six *toises*, but the branches were long and high enough to provide relief from the heat.[1]

The decorated walls and the paradisiacal character of the enclosure are clearly Islamic references. The park of Hesdin established by Robert d'Artois near Arras between 1298 and 1302 would be a perfect illustration of these exotic gardens, especially since he brought back from his Italian sojourn the main elements making up this type of decor. With a perimeter ranging thirteen kilometers, furrowed with canals, enlivened by automata, ornamented with rare flowers, and populated with animals, this place would have significantly eclipsed any fortress-bound gardens.

Throughout the Middle Ages there existed a traditional poetics of the garden as a setting for amorous discourse, a place given over to stanzas and sonnets. Moreover, the first printed anthology treating the poets of the fifteenth century and compiled by a certain Jourdain, is entitled *Le jardin de plaisance et fleur de réthorique*.[2] During this period the castle garden was a miniature realm of enchantment equipped with fountains, hidden water jets, and hydraulic mechanisms, along with raised seats of grassy earth suitable for conversation, bordered with walkways covered by trellised porticos. The ever-square parterres within are planted with medicinal herbs and vegetables chosen for the color of their leaves.

The great thematic renewal of gardens was inspired by an Italian book: Francesco Colonna's *Hypnerotomachia Poliphili* (*Dream of Poliphilus*, 1499), which had a significant impact on the creations of the Renaissance and of seventeenth-century France. It consists above all of a philosophical narrative abounding with enigmas, knotwork, and hieroglyphs, whose solutions and significance the hero investigates and explicates at great length. The sources of inspiration for the dream go back to Egyptian, Etruscan, and Roman antiquity; and the unfolding of the action is a pretext for the description of imaginary spaces where clipped trees and canals mingle with labyrinths and crystal palaces. Although many of these elements were taken up as models and found their way into the projects of the classic age, the fact remains that the work makes no attempt to provide a recipe, carries no aesthetic judgment, establishes no comparison with existing gardens, and (save for a few considerations on the marvels of nature and the use of artifice) is devoid of any theoretical import.

Agronomic treatises reveal a break between the time of the Roman empire and the Renaissance. In her thesis,[3] Martine Gorrichon has noted the absence of original work in this area throughout the Middle Ages, aside from the *Opus ruralium commodorum* by the Bolognese Pietro dei Crescenzi, written between 1304 and 1306, and in 1373 translated into French at the instigation of Charles V under the title *Rustican du labeur des champs*. After referring to the villas of Cicero, Horace, and Pliny, the author undertakes an initial codification of orchards on the basis of the proprietor's social status. He also suggests various planning possibilities and shows how to divide the land into coombs, yards, and orchards outside the surrounding walls.

The sixteenth century, by contrast, saw a flourishing of revivalist works emerging alongside the *Res Rustica*, among which one can cite the *Agriculture et maison rustique* (*Agriculture and rustic mansion*) by Jean Liebault (1564), the *Recepte véritable* (*True recipe*) by Bernard Palissy (1563), and the *Plaisir des champs* (*Pleasure of the Fields*) by Claude Gauchet (1583). It is within the lineage of these works that we should place the *Théâtre d'agriculture et mesnage des champs* (*Theater of Agriculture and Field Care*) by Olivier de Serres, a work that we have already discussed in the context of economic speculation and its links with the political ambitions of Henri IV's government.

De Serres's *Théâtre d'agriculture* is comprised of eight books, of which only the sixth contains a general treatment of gardens. The others treat, successively:

1. The necessity of caretaking (*Du devoir du mesnager*).
2. The working of grain lands.

3. The cultivation of vines.
4. Four-legged livestock.
5. Running a henhouse.
7. Water and wood.
8. The use of food.

It is clear from this summary that we are dealing with a guide for inexperienced farmers, providing indispensable information and reviewing any practical problems that might emerge on a day-to-day basis. Alongside recipes for jams, de Serres gives basic cures for common illnesses and ventures into genetic and medical considerations largely indebted to Aristotle, whose writings were enjoying a significant revival at the time.

Comparison of the Treatises by Olivier de Serres and Boyceau de la Baraudière

The sixth book of de Serres's treatise concerns gardens in general, always from the perspective of their domestic advantages. The title reads *On gardens that provide edible herbs and fruits, fragrant herbs and fruits, medicinal herbs, fruits, trees, saffron, flax, hemp, madder, cloth thistle, reeds, and ways of making partitions to conserve fruits in general.* The book is divided into thirty chapters, of which only four are devoted to pleasure gardens:

10. The *jardin bouquetier* or flower garden, beginning with bushes.
11. Herbs for borders or parterre compartments.
12. Flowers for the *jardin bouquetier.*
13. Use of herbs and flowers for borders and compartments.

The limited interest in the pleasure garden is explicated by a definition provided in the first chapter:

Gardening falls into four types, i.e., the food garden, the flower garden, the medicinal garden, and the fruit garden. . . . [T]he flower garden is composed of all kinds of plants, herbs, flowers, bushes, arranged into compartments in parterres and raised in arches and *cabinets* according to the desires and whims of the Seigneur, more for pleasure than for profit. The one food garden will be larger than the flower and medicinal gardens put together, given that in this place profit is more important than enjoyment.[4]

Already in de Serres one senses a moralizing, almost Puritanical attitude toward those unproductive spaces that fall outside the realm of the edible. In any case, the *Théâtre d'agriculture* contains no hint of the classic garden's references to the categories of beauty and the visual order.

Few seventeenth-century works on agriculture depart from the purely agronomic tendencies that gained momentum with the work of de Serres. Pierre Bétin's *Fidèle jardinier* (1636) or Nicolas Bonnefons's *Jardinier français* (1651) deal only with grafting, manure, and transplantation, skirting any cosmological references and touching only timidly on aesthetic questions. The same can be said of André Mollet's *Jardin de plaisir* (1651) and Claude Mollet's *Théâtre des plans et jardinages* (1652). Although these last two sources are at least distinguished by illustrations of parterres and a global vision approaching the work of Boyceau, they are neither as coherent nor as theoretically compelling.

The 1636 *Traité du jardinage selon les raisons de la nature et de l'art* (*Treatise on gardening according to the rules of nature and art*) reveals its author, Jacques Boyceau de la Baraudière, as an innovator in his domain. The very title bespeaks an intellectual approach to the subject. No French author before him had simultaneously treated philosophical, cosmological, practical, and aesthetic aspects of gardening. But the most interesting fact about this book is that it allows us to perceive the underlying schema of the French garden. Boyceau was a Protestant gentleman who had fought alongside Henri IV. He belonged to the generation of Jean Le Nôtre, whose son André, as we have mentioned, was his subordinate. With this work, the art of gardening acquires disciplinary independence and moves beyond simple horticulturalism. It exemplifies a major shift identical to the one that changed the building trade some fifty years beforehand, when the architect supplanted the master mason and architecture became distinguished from simple construction.

Boyceau hoped that the gardener would be universal in his art: at once agronomist, artist, and scholar. He inscribed his theory of the beautiful garden in the heart of cosmology, founding it on a necessary balance of elements. This search for global coherence through nature assured the validity of his precepts for the general organization of gardens and the sound disposition of parts. Moreover, the book was organized along a logical thread, moving from the laws of nature to the design of gardens by way of arboriculture.

The first book outlines the basic knowledge necessary for understanding the world, with detailed discussions of the air, sea, sun, moon, and seasons. This section ends with two chapters dealing respectively with the qualities required of a gardener and the siting of gardens.[5] The site "is important in three respects; notably in its appearance according to different climates, in the natural fertility of the earth, and in the ease of bringing in water for regular waterings." This definition of the site, greatly influenced by architectural treatises, brings to bear the preceding references to natural history. It also confirms the specific links with geography that provide the groundwork for the establishment of the classic garden.

The second book deals with practical aspects of arboriculture, including pruning, clipping, grafting, and transplanting. The third book, finally, treats "the arrangement and ordering of gardens and of the elements that serve to embellish them." It consists of the following sixteen chapters:

1. That diversity embellishes gardens
2. On the siting of gardens with respect to the lay of the land
3. On the form of gardens
4. On allées and long promenades
5. On parterres
6. On relief
7. On the ways water can be used to embellish a garden
8. On running rivers and brooks
9. On fountains
10. On canals used to carry water to fountains
11. On grottos
12. On aviaries
13. On the types of gardens
14. On the pleasure garden
15. On the utilitarian garden
16. On trellises (*espaliers*)

Among the novelties contained within this outline, we should note first of all the emphasis placed on problems of layout and insertion into the site. There is also a new interest in the renewal of forms and in diversity, subjects to which we will return. Water (evoked here in all its forms) is sufficiently important to take up five out of sixteen chapters, if one includes the theme of grottos. By contrast, strictly utilitarian aspects of the garden are reduced to only two-sixteenths. This change in the balance between utility and pleasure is essential, as it epitomizes the break with tradition and with Olivier de Serres. Nonetheless, as our examination of the Courances archives demonstrates, this is not so much a radical reversal as a restoration of balance. Boyceau can still recommend "that if the prince or other great person making various gardens does not wish to leave the fruits to the mercy of the people in his retinue, it suffices to separate the two."[6] This advice accounts for the continued existence of cultivated lands in the heart of the park in the first half of the century, as opposed to the segregation that will emerge later on, and that Dézallier d'Argenville will echo at the beginning of the eighteenth century.

Whereas Olivier de Serres ultimately addresses himself to a clientele of lesser seigneurs or middling proprietors needing to revive their property, Boyceau de la Baraudière does not hesitate to display a very different set of social ambitions: "If we wish to make gardens that will provide both pleasure and utility, they will not be suited to people of low condition, but only to princes, seigneurs, and gentlemen of means, since beautiful gardens are expensive to create and maintain."[7] This remark confirms that Boyceau's work belongs in the context of the rising class of royal officers from whom he takes his orders.

THE PRECEPTS OF BOYCEAU DE LA BARAUDIÈRE

The precepts and theoretical contributions of Boyceau de la Baraudière center on three main themes: the search for diversity on the level of structure and plan, insertion into the site and adaptation to relief, and the preponderance of water.

Investigations on the Level of the Structure and Plan

Boyceau wished to see a renewal of garden forms. In order to achieve this, he advocated linking his art to drawing: "Just as our first treatises [i.e., the first two parts] depend on a knowledge of the nature and reasons of philosophy, so this one depends on the science of portrayal (*portraiture*), the basis and grounding of all mechanics."[8] He praises the diversity that gives rise to the development of graphic practices: "The most varied gardens will ultimately be considered the most beautiful." This statement implies a move toward complexity, an enriching of composition, the abandonment of the traditional orthogonal grid:

Square forms are the most practical in gardens, be they perfect squares or oblong . . . they contain the straight lines that make allées long and beautiful, and give them a pleasing perspective. But I do not believe that, with all the beauty such straight lines might afford, we should neglect to mix in round and curved forms, or to place oblique forms among the square ones, in order to achieve the variety that nature demands. I would find it most tiresome to see all gardens divided only into straight lines — some divided into four squares, others into nine, others into sixteen — and never to see anything else.[9]

In this plea we find the fundamental schema for the classic garden, clearly distinguished by its use of diagonals and radiating centers. And as we have already suggested, the plotting of angles clearly implies the use of a graphometer.

This evidence provides a clear explanation of the break with the garden forms of the Middle Ages and the Renaissance through the abandonment of the uniform grid structure. The search for variety does not simply affect the plan: it also extends to variations in such factors as the relief, the height of vegetation, the plant species, and the interplay of colors:

I say varied, firstly in the site (*assiette*), then in the general form, in the difference among the various bodies employed, both in the relief and the parterre, in the difference in plants and trees that in and of themselves contain variations in form and color.[10]

This last phrase forcefully evokes compositional principles that can be detected in the landscape paintings of Claude Lorrain or Nicolas Poussin, such as the arrangement and balancing of groupings, or vegetal and chromatic diversity. And so it is that, starting with Boyceau's formulations, the garden acquires the status of landscape.

Insertion into the Site and Adaptation of the Relief

Any consideration of the English garden's insertion into the landscape will invariably acknowledge its unsurpassed mimetic qualities. Yet this same desire for integration seems to appear much sooner in another context. It is Boyceau who introduces an entirely new conception of the garden that, as we have noted, was formulated around the same time in fortifications treatises. There is now a marked interest in adapting to the site, even in difficult circumstances. The constraints encountered by a project are viewed as a stimulus and a source of diversity:

Until now, we have been so preoccupied with equal and uniform sites that we have neglected all others . . . [such as] mountainous and uneven sites in which the nature of the place poses constraints and obstacles; nonetheless, such sites offer other pleasures and commodities that should be valued. . . . Those sites, therefore, that are so happily situated as to combine both kinds of terrain will have a great advantage.[11]

Most gardens in the first half of the seventeenth century (and Courances in particular) are remarkably sensitive to the existing site conditions. Reading Boyceau, we can almost sense the emergence of the taste for steep terrain so characteristic of the picturesque notion of beauty, which has always been set in opposition to the French garden. Irregularity is by no means banished, since the geometric forms of the plan are invariably cast in a supporting role:

Other perfect forms also find their place and their graces in the garden, if they are arranged according to the nature of the place, which is often constrained by mountains, rivers or other impediments, forming pointed or obtuse angles, to which one accommodates the perfect forms that begin within the lines delimiting the area.[12]

Preponderance of Water

The gardens of the first half of the seventeenth century exhibit a subtle use of hydrographic systems, with a marked abundance of basins and canals. According to Boyceau, "the largest expanse of water appears the most beautiful, and its vivacity and movement seems to be the liveliest spirit in a garden; nevertheless, it is best if its grandeur does not efface the other beauties of the garden."[13]

The classic garden is generally thought of as following rigidly defined arrangements. Yet this is not the case, since here, too, everything depends on the context:

Now, when saying in what part of the garden canals should be situated, and how they should be shaped or sized, one cannot make a universal statement: that will depend on the nature of the place and the waters, and partly on whoever is arranging the garden, all of which prevents us from establishing fixed rules.[14]

The choice of a garden site based on natural resources is therefore really the task of the geographer, and includes considerations of hygiene: "We should also add that for the health of the family, it is not good for waters (especially completely stagnant ones) to be too close to the lodgings."

SYMBOLISM OF THE CLASSIC GARDEN AND ORIGINS OF THE CONSTITUTIVE PARTS

Use and Signification

In the first part of this study we considered the evolution of the general composition of gardens in relation to modifications in the château. It now remains to consider the genealogy of the main compositional elements. The symbolism of seventeenth-century gardens is perfectly synchronous with that of the Renaissance. One can detect a consistent philosophy from 1530 to 1640, around which time rationalism begins to replace Aristotelianism. The first Louis XIV style (extending until around 1680 and characterized by Le Brun's profuse interiors of marble, bronze, gilded stucco and mirrors) is bound up with the renascent taste for spectacle. The same holds true of gardens and the ways in which they were used. Hence their essential principles were established well before the time of René Descartes: we should turn above all to Aristotle, Pliny, and the Italian authors of the fifteenth and sixteenth centuries. The interest in the garden theme can be observed in the long romances that were popular in the first half of the century. Châteaux scarcely receive mention here, any more than in memoirs of the period. Gardens, by contrast, are the object of lengthy descriptions, such as the section devoted to Vaux in Madeleine de Scudéry's *Clélie*.

These gardens — and Versailles in particular — were not simply leafy carpets or smooth, regular spaces for promenading. The partial restitution of the great waterworks cannot fully do justice to the site's original potential. True physical extensions of the palace, even in the absence of theatrical representations, these gardens were experienced as a succession of exterior rooms, each offering a different spectacle. The floral decoration was continually updated, when the layouts themselves were not being modified like so many project sketches carried out on the site itself. Nor were they simple festival sites, at least not in the sense that the term is used today. This realm of enchantment went beyond simple spectacle, creating effects in harmony with the worldview of Aristotelian physics.

For the contemporaries of Descartes — indeed, for Descartes himself, if one refers to his book on meteors — the earth was an immense life-form. Hence we should see gardens as privileged points of contact with the magical nature that one was striving to call forth. This helps to explain the taste for metamorphoses, grottoes, knotwork, and water jets tracing the forms of objects as they fall. Granted, we are dealing here with pleasure spots destined for an elite suitably equipped to recognize all of these mythological and cosmological allusions. Yet that which we often perceive as a decor of playful forms divorced from social realities was actually a place devoted to symbolic practices that were taken very seriously, illustrating as they do the aggregate of animist knowledge and beliefs binding the society together. Boyceau's pleasure garden is comprised of

enriched fountains, embellished canals and rivers, grottoes and subterranean areas, aviaries, galleries ornamented with paintings and sculptures, the orangery, better organized allées and walkways, whether covered or uncovered, lawns and fields for ball games and exercise, long alleys for pall-mall games, bosquets, and other raised forms nicely laid out around the parterres or else interspersed inside them, as one sees fit.[15]

Because these compositional elements are confined neither to the French garden nor to Le Nôtre, it will be useful to study the origins of the most important among them, in order to put to rest a certain number of erroneous attributions and false interpretations.

Avenues

Describing the "long roads and allées in the woods and countryside," Boyceau says that the largest seem to be the most beautiful.[16] He also mentions the principle of double rows of trees and contre-alleés. Avenues and forest routes were by no means a novelty in the seventeenth century. While it is true that Sully's administration made some piecemeal efforts to rehabilitate the road network, the decision to line the roads with double rows of elms actually emanated from a decree of Henri II in February 1552:

All lords high justices and all villeins and inhabitants of villages and parishes within each jurisdiction, having to plant and have planted before the end of this present year and in the proper season along the highways and large public roads and in places they will deem most fitting, such a good and large quantity of elms that with the passing of time our kingdom shall be well and sufficiently populated and provided for, and this on pain of arbitrary fine levied by us.[17]

Elsewhere, in Du Chesne's *Antiquités*, we learn that Francis I took great pleasure in Saint-Germain thanks to "the long and wide routes in the neighboring woods, made especially for greater ease and pleasure in hunting stag, boar, and deer."[18] When describing Chambord, the same author evokes the queen's garden, at the end of which, near the Blois forest, there is "an allée six *toises* wide and more than half a league in length embellished with four rows of elms planted six feet apart."[19]

In his chapter devoted to planting on family property, Olivier de Serres recommends that "the homeowner (*ménager*) lay out the avenues of his house for as far as he can with long and wide allées strictly aligned and with a well unified parterre that he will extend through his forests, if possible."[20] The tracing of ample avenues in front of country mansions is therefore not, as is commonly assumed, an invention of André Le Nôtre.

Canals

Pierre Grimal has noted that the great residences of ancient Egypt already incorporated gardens "in which one recognizes certain grand mythical schemas, such as the central canal on which a small boat sails, no doubt a figure of the subterranean sea where the vessel of the sun navigates."[21] In this regard the main reference point (said to have inspired Philibert de l'Orme and fostered the vogue for plans featuring canals) is the Tibertine villa of the emperor Hadrian. This villa, which brought together attributes of many other remarkable sites, was equipped with a large canal (lined with porticoes and giving onto a sanctuary) called *Canopus* in reference to the Canopic Valley.[22] This *Canopus*, and the Tibur villa in general, were a great inspiration for the *Hypnerotomachia Poliphili*, in which the hero generally travels by aquatic routes. Yet we should not overlook the connection between garden canals and efforts to connect various rivers in the late sixteenth and early seventeenth centuries. When we examine Versailles, we will see a clear intersection of these two aspects of a single phenomenon.

The importance of water in the classic landscape is derived from its obvious economic advantage as a means of transportation: poor road conditions contributed to the predominance of travel by water routes along the rivers and coastlines. With Richelieu, the seventeenth century also saw the emergence of a clear desire to establish a naval policy.[23] Water constantly appears as a theme in Baroque romances, and for the Grand Canal at Versailles Colbert ordered nine small boats to be made in Rouen, and on the site itself he built a galliot armed with thirty-two cannons. Alongside this were various gifts from foreign powers: a Neapolitan felucca, two gondolas given by the Venetian doge, and a galley. Sixty sailors were permanently at the ready, living in a nearby village built to house them.

In the novels of Madeleine de Scudéry there is an insistence on gushing and bubbling water, but for the most part seventeenth-century poetry exhibits a strong preference for fresh waters, like the lake or fountain forming a mirror that both enhances and disrupts the projected image. This taste for reflections can be explained on a philosophical level as a rendering of the ephemerality of things, and it should be linked to the investigations and optical oddities that filled curiosity cabinets, such as distorting prisms and lenses. To this illusionistic universe we should add the galleries and intimate rooms fitted with mirrors that made the outside landscape suddenly appear inside of houses.[24]

Looking up *canal* in Furetière's *Dictionnaire*, one finds the following four definitions:

1. The bed of a river or stream made by nature for water to flow through.
2. Artificial conduits dug into the earth, either to connect rivers with each other or to weaken them when their current is too strong.
3. Water conduits made to embellish gardens, most often revetted with stone.

Figure 14. The Marais d'Eau and the Montagne d'Eau at Versailles, from Gabriel Pérelle, *Plus beaux lieux de France et d'Italie* (Paris: Bibliothèque des Arts Décoratifs).

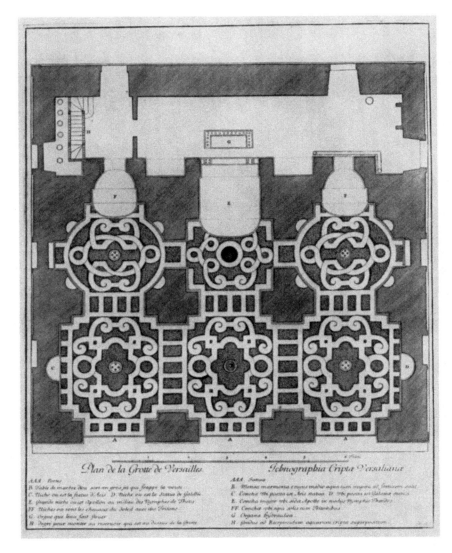

4. Small conduits that naturally occur in the earth, through which spring waters run, and metal ore rises.

This last definition is especially interesting, since it shows canals to be at the heart of natural history as it was then conceived. In the seventeenth century lakes were considered the eyes of the ocean, with which they were connected by way of subterranean conduits. This idea comes from Aristotle and reappears in the *Meteors* of Descartes. Springs are thus resurgences of the sea, and all waters communicate. Here the water systems feeding garden basins and fountains appear as the complements of a planetary hydraulic system, and hence as participants in a whole subterranean world.

Grottos

The underground world was actually a main center of interest in the culture of the seventeenth century. It receives abundant treatment in works such as the *Mundus subterraneus* of the German Jesuit Athanasius Kircher, or that of Jacques, Sieur de Gaffarel.[25] The latter work constitutes a veritable inventory of every type of cavity that one could encounter: grottos, caves, lairs, abysses, quagmires, mines, crypts, underground cities — nothing is left out of his enumeration. All the caverns he describes fall into the following five categories: divine, human, brutal, natural, and artificial. To this last category belong the garden caverns that Boyceau de la Baraudière describes as made

to represent savage caves, whether cut into natural rock or expressly built somewhere else: in addition, they are built somber and somewhat obscure. They are ornamented with rustic objects (spongy rocks, boulders, multicolored pebbles, fossils [*pétrifications*], shells). With water as well, one can activate engines and machines. Gutters and splashing water are fitting and most seemly, making things more natural. One can place paintings here, or paint frescoes on the walls. The paintings that we call grotesques were invented by the ancients for this purpose; some of them can still be seen in certain underground antiquities in which are counterfeited animals and other representations of extravagant forms and gestures, some natural and others going against nature so as to render these places all the more bizarre.

Figure 15. Plan and façade of the Grotto of Thetis, Versailles, from André Félibien, *Description de la grotte de Versailles* (Paris: Imprimérie Royale, 1679).

16a

Figure 16 a–c. Costume embroidery, botanical illustrations, and parterres de broderies all participate in a general tendency toward vegetal abstraction. Costume from the Maciet collection. Botanical illustration from Pierre Vallet, *Le jardin du roy très chrestien Henry IV* (1608). Method for tracing parterres as depicted in Dézallier d'Argenville, *Théorie et pratique du jardinage* (1747).

Predating the grottos at Wideville, Saint-Germain, Meudon, Vaux, and Versailles, the first example of this type of edifice known in France is the Grotto of the Pines at Fontainebleau, built in 1543–44 at one end of the Gallery of Ulysses. According to Louis Hautecoeur, there had been a precedent between 1527 and 1540 in the Parc de Pagny, then owned by the admiral Chabot.[26] In any case, such places refer to the myth of the origins of life, and more precisely to the grotto at Praeneste called the Lair of the Fates. This natural grotto, opening onto a hillside, had been considered a sacred place since the seventh century B.C. The emperor Hadrian had it decorated with a mosaic depicting the appearance of life on earth out of a watery medium.[27]

The Parterres de broderies

Knotwork and arabesque forms belong to a historical grammar of the visual arts whose origins are difficult to determine.[28] The Orient is usually mentioned in this context, but it would be wrong to see the diffusion as following in the wake of the Crusades, since this type of ornament appeared long before in such elements as the spirals and rolls of Roman grillwork, hinges, and capitals. It also appeared in Celtic metalwork, particularly Irish work from the sixth century B.C. According to Boyceau de la Baraudière, "Parterres are the low form of garden embellishment that are extremely graceful, especially when viewed from an elevation," a remark reminding us that this consideration did not originate with Le Nôtre. Boyceau goes on to

16b   16c

say that parterres "are made with borders of many shrubs and undergrowth of various colors, fashioned in a different manner, with compartments, foliage, braids, moresques, arabesques, guilloches, rosettes, glorioles, targes, escutcheons, ciphers, and devices." [29]

Parterres de broderies were already in use by the sixteenth century, as we can see from the plates by du Cerceau, notably the ones representing the châteaux of Gaillon and Amboise. It is unlikely that the architect Étienne Dupérac invented this form. On the contrary, it would be more reasonable to associate such broderies with the sixteenth-century surge in botany, which heralded in a widespread movement of graphic transcription and abstraction of the vegetal order. The proliferation of gardens specializing in plant taxonomy is an important sign of this evolution. The ladies of the court visited the garden on the Ile Nôtre-Dame seeking models for their embroidery. In response to this demand, Pierre Vallet, embroiderer to the king, put together a collection of designs for use in decoration. Hence there are close links among costume embroidery, botanical plates, and parterre designs.

Over the course of the seventeenth century, one can observe a modification of parterre designs in the direction of more simplified lines and a more graphic presence on the terrain—features that also make for easier maintenance. Claude Mollet's parterre designs illustrating the *Théâtre d'agriculture* by Olivier de Serres

LIEV SIXIESME. 597

C'EST VN COMPARTIMENT DE CEVX
DES NOVVEAVX IARDINS DV ROI AVX
Tuilleries, faifant vn carreau, dont les vuïdes font
remplis d'enrichiffemens, au centre duquel
eft vne deuife du Roi.

Figure 17. Parterre by Claude Mollet, from Olivier de Serres, *Théâtre d'agriculture* (1603).

bear comparison with du Cerceau's plates. They appear as a marquetry of surfaces arranged in radial symmetry, enclosing fleurons or spiraling rolls. With Boyceau de la Baraudière there is a move away from marquetry toward calligraphy, with branching lines of upward and downward strokes, conceived on a greater scale and suggesting wrought-iron work. With Le Nôtre the design increases in thickness and presence; the figures define the contour, and the linking of forms is more logical. As Dézallier d'Argenville advises, "in order to be beautiful, broderie must be light,

Figure 18. Parterre by Boyceau de Baraudière.

easily understood and free of confusion," and at the same time one must avoid falling "into the opposite extreme, namely making the parterres so lightly that they
are completely unadorned and have such a weak and thin *broderie* that they do not
figure prominently enough on the ground, so that one has to pull them up four or
five years later, when the lines of boxwood run together and become embroiled."[30]

Above the level of boxwood arabesques, classic gardens frequently included
topiary art consisting of trees cut into architectural forms or genre scenes. This is
part of a Roman gardening tradition revived by the *Hypnerotomachia poliphili*.

COMPARATIVE STUDY OF SOME GARDENS FROM
THE FIRST HALF OF THE SEVENTEENTH CENTURY

The term "classic garden" invariably evokes an image of rigid order and fussy uniformity based on strict formulas and immutable forms. According to traditional

Figure 19. Parterre by Dézallier d'Argenville, *Théorie et pratique du jardinage* (1747).

art history, Vaux is a canonical type marking the emergence of a new style: a revolutionary way of distributing space, uncommon until that point. Yet an analysis of the constitutive parts and their relations to the gardens of the preceding years reveals that this is not at all the case. There is an immediately discernible diversity resulting from a concern for contextual adaptation. One can distinguish two types of projects in this regard: those that take advantage of the physical environment while largely respecting its morphology, and those that radically modify it. The first type of intervention, which could be described as mild, generally characterizes the years 1600–1660, whereas large-scale operations giving rise to modern planning techniques correspond to the reign of Louis XIV.

In any case it is not possible to establish a fixed archetype of the classic garden; at least in the early stages, this way of treating the landscape cannot be reduced to a single model. At most we can discern a certain number of ways of dealing with the surrounding space. Since there is great diversity in the handling of details, we must limit ourselves to observing similarities and kinships, and not try to infer absolute rules. And yet we can observe a clear evolution of layouts over the decades, revealed in the increasing complexity of networks.

Seventeenth-century drawings for park designs are extremely rare. Land-use maps were not drawn up immediately, and with few exceptions eighteenth-century plans were privately acquired. Only the Cassini hunting map allows for comparison on a constant scale. Although this map was drawn up a good hundred years after the establishment of the gardens under discussion here, we should keep in mind that there were minimal modifications in the intervening years. During the eighteenth century, gardens tended either to preserve their original structure or else to be recast in an Anglo-Chinese style, hence there is minimal risk of error. The existing lineaments are usually in place by 1700. At Courances, for example, notarial documents indicate no further acquisitions of land for the park. The collected descriptions from the Enlightenment are further evidence of this tendency to settle into a fixed form. The surviving administrative plans provide invaluable documentation, since their polychromatic treatment gives a faithful image of the composition of parks and the allotment of space.

We will begin the present inquiry by focusing on the area within what is now the Département of Essonne—a choice dictated partly by professional convenience, but also by the concentration of residences and the existence of a large number of administrative plans.[31] This will be followed by a critical analysis of the domains of Lemours, Mesnilvoisin, Grosbois, Rosny,[32] Courances, Chilly, La Grange, and Evry. Taken as a whole, this documentation will enable us to construe the developments at Vaux in terms of continuity rather than rupture. I have used the following criteria:

1. Orientation, relation to relief, and hydrography
2. Relation to the built environment
3. Form of the contour, general positioning, and the road system
4. Positioning of elements and proportional distribution of spaces

Orientation, Relation to Relief and Hydrography

The royal hunting map reveals an indisputable preference for two orientations. The main axis is generally northeast-southwest or northwest-southeast. The concentration of water was a major influence on the choice of composition. River sites invited two possible solutions: as in the case of Rosny, one could trace a great axis parallel to the river bed providing lateral views extending out from the residence, a treatment that is especially felicitous on flat terrain. The preferred solution was to establish a great perpendicular axis, as François Mansart did at Maisons and Evry-petit-Bourg. This second solution, better suited to the creation of stepped terraces terminating in a type of belvedere jutting out into the water, became a common arrangement, and is evident at Juvisy and especially at Choisy. This relationship to the water was to prove extremely influential, as witnessed by the fact that formations lacking such a proximity recreated it by means of large artificial canals, whether lateral (Courances, Chilly) or transverse (Vaux).

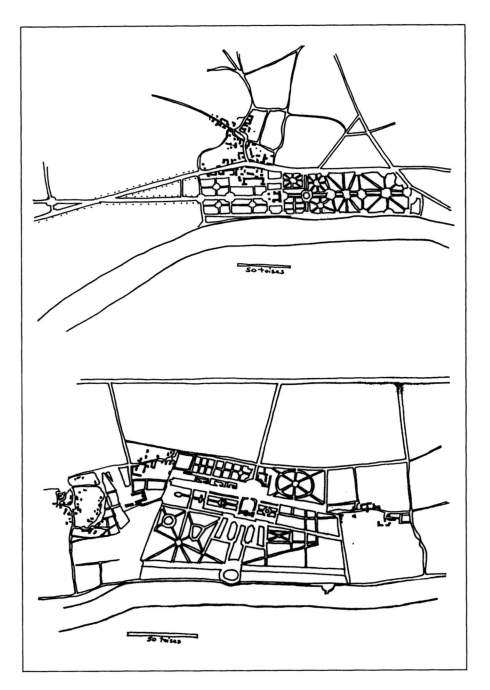

Figure 20. Rosny and Evry-petit-Bourg (the latter by François Mansart), indicating the two types of orientation in relation to a river. The organization along a major perpendicular axis, also evident at Maisons, is ultimately employed at Choisy.

No less important are other hydrographic elements, including small waterways, rivers, and springs. These features also determine the choice of composition. The canal systems that we will examine are often nothing more than the enlargement of such systems, to which stone coping gives an architectonic character. Courances, situated between a network of springs and the river Ecole, is revealed on the administrative plans as the final stage of this type of exploitation of the site's aquatic potential. Leaving aside these skilful if uneconomical solutions, we discover that the gardens of this period resort only to very sober effects motivated by the existing relief. In the final analysis, they are nothing more than discrete interventions into the environment.

Relation to the Built Environment

One of the constant features of this insertion of gardens into the site is a respect for rural villages. Far from being threatened or reallocated, such settlements often plainly overlap the garden (Chilly, Rosny). At the very least, they are placed at a far end of the garden (Evry) or in some explicit relation to it (Courances). In cases where an isolated settlement arises, as at the château of La Grange at Yerres, there is no sign of prior eviction.

Form of the Contour, General Positioning, and the Road System

Although the exterior forms of these gardens do not follow fixed rules, we can often discern a principle of converging contour lines. The convergence is never fully realized, since the most characteristic forms at Chilly and La Grange achieve a trapezoidal form. Aside from these two examples (which might at most suggest that some kind of model was followed) the general layout, including the configuration of the exterior envelope, tends to follow the relief and adapt to the conditions of the site, in accordance with Boyceau's prescriptions. In such cases the polygonal layout retains the principles of convergence already observed, though adapted to a specific context. This arrangement is evident at Courances, where the river Ecole serves as a wedge and the center of the village as a means of articulation. A general feature of this period is the lack of extension into the space beyond, except in isolated cases like the château of La Grange, where the avenue also serves as a thoroughfare. Hence gardens do not yet have radiating road systems.

None of the gardens examined so far exhibits a flagrant bilateral symmetry. It is more accurate to speak of a *principal axis* and *central space*. This axis clearly passes through the center of the residence, establishing a dominant pathway. What we call the *central space* complies, at least on the level of the envelope, with a rule of symmetry. Evry is a clear example of such an approach. Yet we should bear in mind that a plan showing a symmetrical central space might have a very different

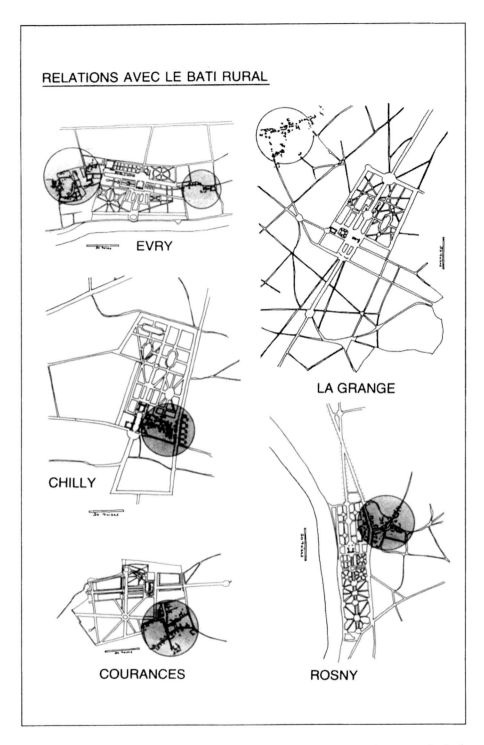

Figure 21. Evry, Chilly, Courances, La Grange d'Yerres, and Rosny—relations to the built environment.

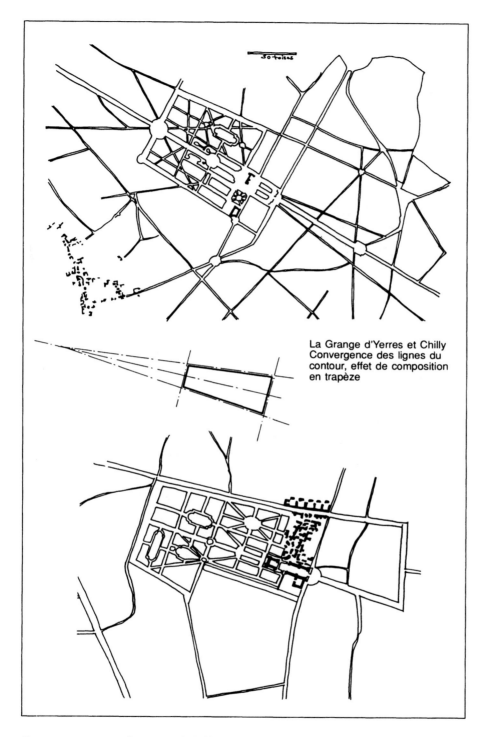

La Grange d'Yerres et Chilly
Convergence des lignes du
contour, effet de composition
en trapèze

Figure 22. La Grange d'Yerres and Chilly — convergence of contour lines resulting in a trapezoidal configuration.

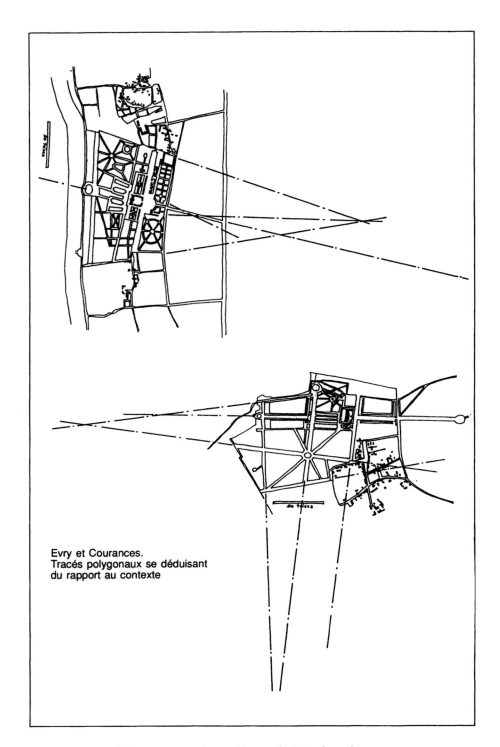

Evry et Courances.
Tracés polygonaux se déduisant
du rapport au contexte

Figure 23. Evry and Courances — polygonal layout deriving from the context.

effect in elevation, as is the case at Chilly. There the parterres on the left respond to the masses of trees on the right, which are similarly shaped in order to provide a lateral view across the canal. The same spirit is evident at Rosny, where the fore-park is treated freely, with notable differences in the size of the parterres on either side of the axis.

Positioning of Elements and Proportional Distribution of Spaces

If one considers the massing of high and low vegetation, it is clear that forests dominate the distance and that the parterres serve as a type of clearing. Moreover, the great enclosures of the early seventeenth century are essentially parks designed to contain game, a function very much in evidence in the plans of Limours, Mesnilvoisin, and Grosbois. The main lines of the design are a network of forest allées that become increasingly complex as the function of the woods as hunting-ground gives way to the promenade; the vegetal covering dotted with bosquets then becomes a kind of vast labyrinth. In all three sites the garden proper is severely curtailed, at most occupying the immediate surroundings of the residence. Similarly, the proportional relations among the allées are determined by the complexity of the system, and we can discern a hierarchy involving a principal network of large axes, a secondary network of parallel axes, and a tertiary, diagonal network.

Yet in the cases of Courances, Evry, Rosny, and Chilly there is a different configuration. Here the central space, and the low vegetation in particular, gains in importance. The administrative plan for Courances reveals an unhindered handling of the central space, with the symmetry ultimately confined to the area along the principal axis, all other areas being treated with great freedom. A screen of trees, cutting through the middle of the park and pierced at the center, appears from the distance as a kind of aperture; passing through it, one reenters a flat space interspersed with canals.

There is also an aperture effect in the central space at Evry, but here the marked dilation distinguishes it from the others, relating it to subsequent compositions. Notarial descriptions indicate an essentially bipartite organization, with a *petit parc* before the residence and a larger one in back. Nonetheless, at Rosny, Courances, and Evry, one observes a clear three-part division along a plan parallel with the façade.

CRITICAL ANALYSIS OF COURANCES

It is generally conceded that French gardens from the Renaissance to Vaux-le-Vicomte produced nothing of great significance. This attitude results from traditional stylistic periodization, with its sudden births and radical transformations by innovative individuals. Yet we have seen how, on the contrary, the first half of the seventeenth century was a period of unprecedented development in this domain,

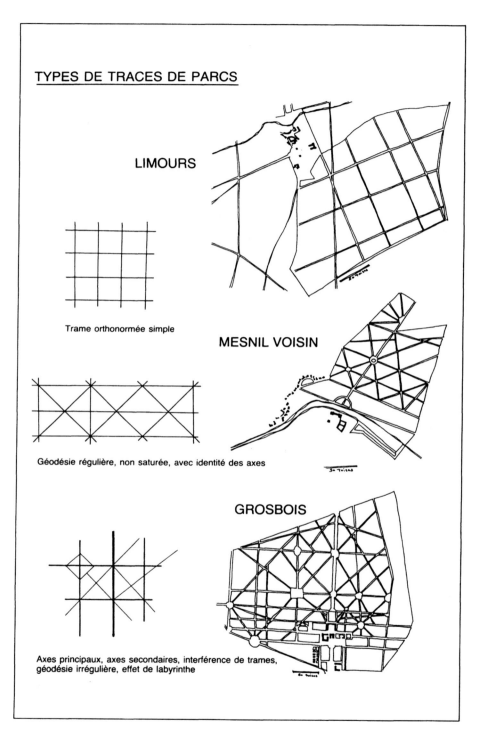

TYPES DE TRACES DE PARCS

LIMOURS

Trame orthonormée simple

MESNIL VOISIN

Géodésie régulière, non saturée, avec identité des axes

GROSBOIS

Axes principaux, axes secondaires, interférence de trames, géodésie irrégulière, effet de labyrinthe

Figure 24. Types of park layouts. Limours, a simple orthogonal grid; Mesnilvoisin, regular divisions, not extremely dense, equal emphasis on all axes; Grosbois, primary and secondary axes, interpenetrating schemas, irregular divisions, labyrinth effect.

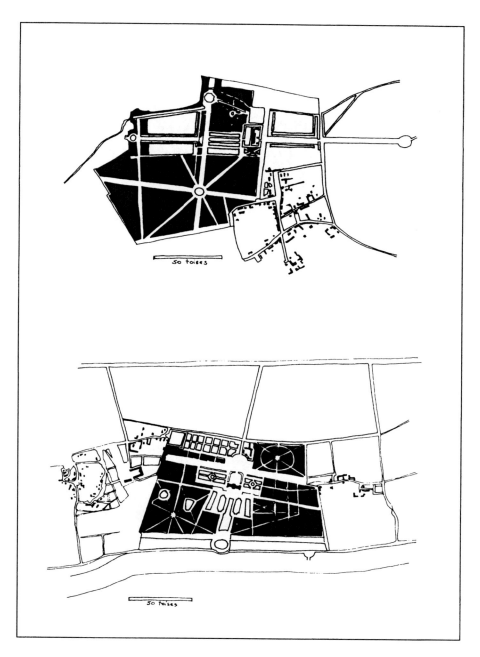

Figure 25. Courances and Evry—composition and relation of areas of vegetation, based on the administrative plan.

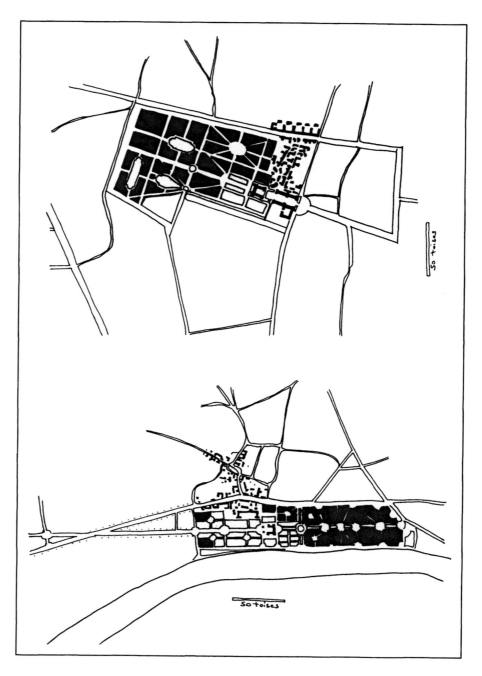

Figure 26. Chilly and Rosny—composition and relation of areas of vegetation, based on the administrative plan.

both in terms of conceptualization and in the number of projects realized. For this reason, before asking whether Vaux marks a significant departure in the history of gardens, it will be helpful to extend our analysis of the Courances park, and, working our way back through successive phases, to reveal the structure of a garden whose general composition dates back to before 1630.

Exploitation of the Site and Its Resources

Dézallier d'Argenville can be credited with establishing the discourse on hydrology as well as art criticism.[33] He notes that the water system at Courances presented a great deal of potential, and that the park's most original feature is its exploitation of this potential:

It is the whiteness (*blancheur*) and the current (*courant*) of the waters in this beautiful place that gave it the name Courances. Their clarity is such that one can distinctly see the most beautiful trout at the bottom of the canal.... [T]his chateau is surrounded by two moats fed by two streams. To its right is an almost square *pièce d'eau* [the fishpond], enclosed by fourteen dolphins, each spouting enough water to turn a mill. These still waters come from the river Ecole that passes through the park along the walls....[A]ll of these waters flow night and day, without any reservoirs or spouts. It is nature stripped of all art: nothing is lacking in this garden except a decent view.

This last phrase is most interesting, since it contains both a thinly veiled critique of the artifice at Versailles and a recognition by eighteenth-century naturalists (in a text dated 1755) of the exceptional status of Courances in relation to the then muchcriticized principles of the French garden. And yet, crucially, Dézallier d'Argenville laments the lack of a view. Indeed, despite a slight natural declivity on the transverse axis in the direction of the river Ecole, the park of Courances is completely level from the entry gate to the semicircular terrace terminating the composition at the end of the main axis. This general flatness, along with the high proportion of covering vegetation, would be evidence enough (if one needed it) to refute the intervention of André Le Nôtre, who is known from early descriptions to have had a taste for clarity, the interplay of various levels, and views into the distance.

On the other hand, comparison of the descriptions furnished by Dézallier d'Argenville reveals a key similarity between Courances and Liancourt, a work by Jacques Boyceau de la Baraudière. This similarity lies in the use of access canals and double canals, in addition to the fact that both parks derive their effects from adjoining rivers. At Courances the avenue leading to the forecourt is "enhanced by two canals with dolphins at their head."[34] At Liancourt "facing the gateway of the château one finds the canal of the Mall" and after the terrace descent comes "a *parterre d'eau* made up of two very long pieces.... [T]his parterre runs into a large meadow surrounded by a double row of canals and poplars imported from Flanders."[35]

The hydraulic installations at Courances are in every way comparable to this: we can compare the multiple basins, the Grand Canal lined with poplars, the reflecting pond facing the château, and the two parallel canals bordering the second part of the main axis. The latter features have since disappeared, but they are clearly visible on the administrative plan.

Historical Validity of the Existing Site: Losses and Additions

Due to a series of vicissitudes (prolonged abandonment, an idealizing nineteenth-century restoration, and damage during the World War II Occupation), the château and park of Courances have suffered losses in relation to early descriptions, despite the extreme care of the present owners to maintain a faithful historical appearance.

Whereas the Vaux gardens have been almost entirely restored, those at Courances provide only the broadest sense of this original state, very evocative yet somewhat lost in the onslaught of greenery. This is the case with almost all of our classic parks, which are overrun with proliferous vegetation on the model of Chateaubriand's *Atala*. By classical standards the anglicizing romanticism of park managers in the previous century is an aberration, since in the seventeenth century nature was regarded as something to be regulated, sliced up, and dominated. Today we know that the foliage at Versailles would have to be pruned back to half its height, given the earlier refusals to trim it at regular intervals.

At Courances the stylistic ambiguity is more fundamental, since it seems that the general treatment of the allées as carpets of greenery (even in the wooded areas) is a preservation of the original situation rather that a concession to naturalism. This is certainly the best solution given the abundance of water and the spongy quality of the soil, since it is the only way to achieve a satisfying appearance in all weather conditions: stabilized soil, sand, packed earth, or gravel could only enjoy a temporary existence at Courances. Instead, the ubiquitous vegetation gives a somewhat magical impression, sweeping us up in a material continuum where soil, arbor, woods, and foliage run together. Only the unswerving linearity of the allées reminds us that we are not in a forest, but rather in a domesticated space corresponding perfectly to the seventeenth-century notion of a *parc*.

Courances is a prime example of a work that has been modified, and yet remains coherent enough for the alterations not immediately to upset the view. Their importance becomes clear when we compare the very beautiful administrative plan, preserved in the archives of the Département of Yvelines, with a modern map. These discrepancies notwithstanding, the perimeter of the property turns out to be the same as it was two hundred years ago, and the general configuration remains unchanged. The right side of the park (the largest surface when seen from a distance) is in the course of being replanted, and the large forest allées clearly visible on the eighteenth-century document are now reduced to a few rugged pathways. When considering this locale we should keep in mind that the explosion of a

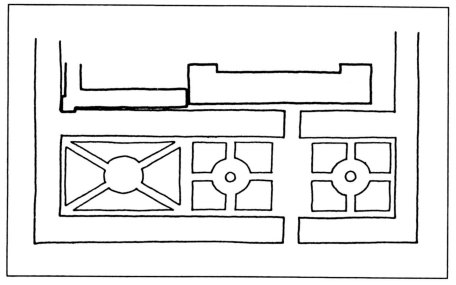

Figure 27. The present Courances parterres (photo) do not correspond to the layout on the administrative plan (drawing).

munitions depot during World War II led to the almost total destruction of the old woodlands.

Despite the replacement of the elms with chestnut trees in 1782, the small access park has scarcely changed. By contrast, the *corps de logis* has undergone some additions that entailed raising the grand stairway and the adjoining structures. Fortunately, excessive restorations by the architect Destailleur (notably the hyper-baroque detailing on the dormer level) have recently been toned down. Thanks to the efforts of Messieurs de Ganay, father and son, the château now exhibits a respectable simplicity in keeping with the spirit of early prints. To the side of the moats, the neoclassical landscape designer Achille Duchêne has left evidence of his work on the grounds, in the form of a semicircular basin fed by a fountain with a statue of Diana believed to have come from Marly. Still, however harmonious this arrangement might be overall, the addition of chestnut quincunxes constitutes an archaeological error because of its excessive proximity to the residence.

Entering the moat enclosure behind the *corps de logis*, we find a small garden that is deplorably misconceived from an art historical perspective. Here the two parterres with boxwood arabesques were redesigned in the last century, in keeping with the image of Le Nôtre promoted in Dézallier d'Argenville's treatise. In any case, it has nothing to do with the original arrangement. Other designs can be found in the print by Israël Henriet (see Figure 9, p. 25), the administrative plan (see Figure 7, p. 22), and the large plan preserved by Jean-Louis de Ganay. A secondary moat had originally extended along the level of the rear façade, making this garden into an island approached by means of drawbridges. A break in the level of the existing balustrade confirms the accuracy of this allusion to the *Hypnerotomachia Poliphili*. The parterres in the print by Israël Silvestre are bipartite and embellished with yews. The administrative plan and the plan at the château depict these parterres as three squares segmented by diagonal lines. These last features are only weakly indicated on the print, which would have been made in the studio on the basis of a few site sketches; as a result it tends to reduce the parterre to a few graphic symbols. Turning to the center and right side of the Grand Parc, we can lament the disappearance of three supporting canals that together would have made this water system a truly unique ensemble.

THE ORIGINALITY OF VAUX

We know that in his youth André Le Nôtre worked not only in the Tuileries but also in the Luxembourg Gardens. On the other hand, nothing is known of his collaboration with François Mansart, and Dézallier d'Argenville, in his 1755 *Voyage pittoresque des environs de Paris*, cites Gagny as his first work.[36] Jean Cordey, working in the Vaux archives early in this century, could not determine exactly when Le Nôtre had been engaged by Nicolas Fouquet, nor could he find the ledger for the Vaux commission. Moreover the original plan has been lost, and there is no trace of the contracts and estimates for Le Nôtre's work for Fouquet. Despite these gaps, the paternity of the garden is beyond doubt. And even though it is not certain (as we have just shown) that Vaux was Le Nôtre's first complete work, an analysis of the garden will certainly help us place the specific features of his style in relation to the earlier gardens examined here.

Orientation, Relation to Relief and Hydrography

For its major axis Vaux uses one of two orientations traditionally employed by earlier gardens: northwest-southeast. The Cassini map (Figure 28) shows how this park is deliberately made to straddle the valley in which the river Monceaux, momentarily transformed into the Grand Canal, serves as a caesura in the composition. Once again we see a flagrant exploitation of the existing site, confirming the impact of Boyceau's precepts.

Relation to the Built Environment

In comparison with gardens made before the classic era, Vaux relates to the pre-existing seigneurial and village habitat in a brutally innovative manner. Around 1635 François Fouquet purchased a small domain named Vaux in the parish of Maincy. His son Nicolas purchased the entire seigneurie in 1641. This comprised an ancient seigneurial residence surrounded by a moat, along with its dependencies, a chapel, and four water mills. The nearby hamlet of Jumeaux was joined to this ensemble. In 1656 Nicolas Fouquet purchased the fields, vineyards, and meadows necessary for the realization of his immense project, along with the hamlet of Maison-Rouge. After the expropriation of the residents, the two areas of rural inhabitation were pitilessly razed along with the existing seigneurial settlement.

Erasing an existing habitat in order to create a park is a key innovation, opening the way to planning policies that go beyond private interests in favor of a more territorial outlook. This notion of a tabula rasa initiates a new mode of thinking that will become the way of centralized power. The Versailles project represents an initial step in this direction.

Form of the Contour, General Positioning, and the Road System

The composition of Vaux is based entirely on its perpendicular relation to the stream and recurs in the orthogonal system of the overall design, where only the two extremities radiate. Cassini's map of France shows how the three linking roads branch out across the two short sides of the rectangle, and also along a transverse axis, following a logic of circulation based on ridge routes and valley routes. The

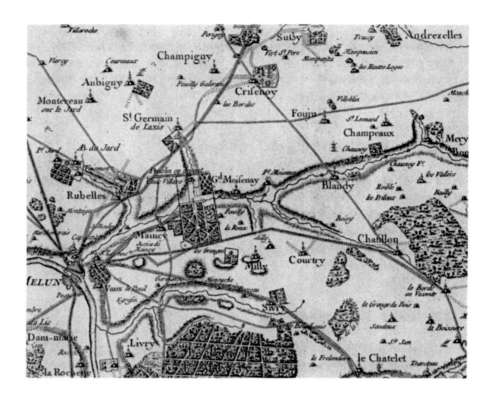

Figure 28. Location of Vaux-le-Vicomte on Cassini's map; comparison with Courances on the same scale.

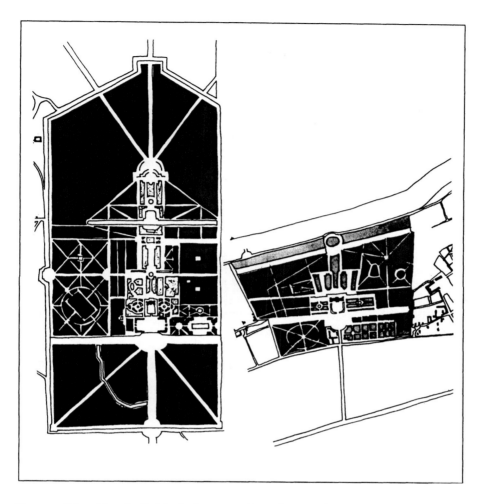

Figure 29. Disturbing similarities in the conceptions of Evry and Vaux.

overall design is necessarily asymmetrical in relation to the main axis, as is the handling of details. Only the buildings and the central space delimited by the wooded front exhibit a bilateral symmetry.

The major organizational choices behind this composition are disturbingly similar to the ones used some years earlier by François Mansart at Evry-petit-Bourg (Figure 29). Here we find the same transverse tripartite division, the same clearing around the residence, the same aperture effect achieved by a contraction of the central space, and the same opening onto an aquatic channel (the Seine in one case, the canal in the other). Not to mention the different levels and the interplay of terraces that constitutes the originality of Evry, and that reappear at Vaux. These features reveal a genuine influence, confirming the terms of a short text discovered by Alan Braham and Peter Smith among the manuscripts in the Bibliothèque Nationale relating to the youth of Jules-Hardouin Mansart:

There was never any other like Monsieur Le Nostre, whose superior genius enabled him to far outstrip all of those who had previously practiced his profession; and we can say that the late Monsieur Mansart, the uncle [sic. (great uncle)] of the man whom I am endeavoring to speak about today, contributed in no small way, by his teachings and his lessons like the great architect that he was, to giving ideas to the aforesaid Monsieur Le Nostre; and I have learned that he did so with all the more pleasure in that he found him to be capable of profiting from these lessons. And however great the talents of Monsieur Le Nostre, he cannot deny his indebtedness to the infinite talents of the late Monsieur Mansart.[37]

Positioning of Elements and Proportional Distribution of Spaces

The tripartite division of Vaux is clearly discernible in Figure 30. The access park is succeeded by the garden, and then by the upper park. Far from being separate sequences, these three large sections link together and overlap one another. The inflection of the main axis, combining an initial plunging view, a rise, and then a somewhat flatter vista, is clearly a perspectival effect derived from the morphology of the site. Whether or not as a result of this experience, Le Nôtre's work always tends to break the linearity and monotony with a play of different levels, landings, and inflections. In the chapter devoted to fortifications, we also saw that his tendency to cut into the earth and his arrangement that allows one to scour the earth at a glance reveal a knowledge of military engineering.

On closer inspection, we can see that the middle section, or garden space, is built on a rectangular framework that seems to spread into the distance. This reference to the structure of the great urban royal gardens is hardly inconsequential. It is the very foundation of this work's originality, as we will soon see in more detail.

Conclusions About the Vaux Affair

Fouquet's work at Vaux was a genuine piece of planning (aménagement). He had already pursued the subject on various fronts—notably at Belle-Isle—and the inventory of his house at Saint-Mandé lists a large number of geography books. His own intentions eventually overshadowed the interests of the state, leading to a downfall that was more than a personal defeat: it signaled the end of an age in which the financiers, with their country mansions, had been masters of powerful landowning operations. It is clear that such large-scale planning could not be left in their hands for long. The meal for six thousand guests catered by Vatel and the Italian-style lottery in which jewelry, costumes, prize weaponry, and even purebred horses were given away marked the apotheosis of an era. These features made

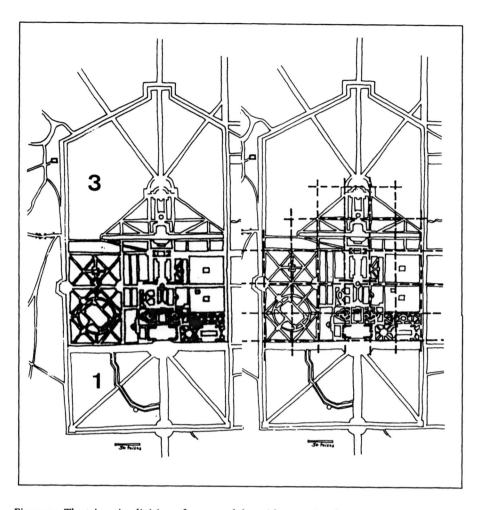

Figure 30. The tripartite division of space and the grid governing the composition at Vaux.

Vaux into a type of immense potlatch, which mired the hopes of a social class that had become a nuisance on account of its excessive power.

FRAGMENTS OF LE NÔTRE'S THEORY
AND TYPICAL FEATURES OF HIS STYLE

Is it such a great loss that André Le Nôtre did not write a single theoretical work? It is hard to think otherwise: the gardens themselves would be sufficient testimony to his approach only if its limits were better defined, or if restorations had not brought important modifications of detail. As it stands, any classical-looking garden is now attributed to him, and the term *jardin à Le Nôtre* is frequently bandied about. Such is the price of his success, his merits, and the place assigned to him by eager historians—yet we must not be taken in by this. Despite enormous gaps, we do possess a few pieces of information and testimony providing a fairly precise idea of Le Nôtre's conceptions. In addition, the treatise by Dézallier d'Argenville that appeared some years after his death seems to be a compilation of scattered principles and reflections gleaned from Le Nôtre or his immediate circle.

Refinement of the Composition

Le Nôtre was not innovative in his exploitation of a given site, nor in the general schema of the classic garden. These two aspects of the problem were part of the culture that shaped him, as we saw in the consideration of numerous examples preceding his own work. What Le Nôtre did supply was a considerable enrichment of garden forms, due in all likelihood to the experience of his youth. His organizational prowess, including the ability to establish a marked spatial differentiation in a given place, becomes evident when one compares his intervention in the Tuileries gardens with the original plan of 1580. The same observation can be made with his work at Versailles. The underlying framework that we have detected at Vaux is characteristic of his technique. Here the process of reducing the space to a grid is carried out with such skill that it is imperceptible to the eye, which is diverted by the presence of alternating and mediating secondary lines that run parallel, diagonal, or in some other direction.

Le Nôtre's personal style is characterized by an ability to produce interlocking compositions in which each level constitutes a search for complexity. His procedure seems to be as follows: having established the orientation lines that are a function of the site, he lays out the general composition in the form of a linear framework that he then divides into sections. Within each section he adopts different types of direction lines, onto which are superimposed patterns of void and solid, or variations in the relative density of vegetation. At Vaux, for example, the middle third of the park is governed by a single grid, but the expressions vary: the left-hand side involves a play of diagonals and the superimposition of networks onto expanses of high vegetation, whereas the central section exhibits irregular longitudinal divisions, along with the mixing of parterres with ground cover. The right-hand side, finally, adopts a composition made up of rectangular wooded areas extending at right angles to the main axis. These divisions remain arbitrary, with the three parts interpenetrating thanks to transitions that blur changes in the layout.

This composition clearly explores notions of zonage, threshold, and transition. While the plan is deliberately continuous, there are marked differences in elevation, and in the distribution of masses from the central space with its parterres, through the bosquets, and on into the deep woods. The result of this progression is an effect of coherence but also of crescendo, amounting to a kinesthetic sensation of rigorous equilibrium.

Primacy of the General Concept

Saint-Simon reports that Le Nôtre said parterres "were good only for nannies who couldn't leave their charges, walking through them with their eyes and admiring them from the second floor." He adds that Le Nôtre "excelled in them nonetheless, as in all parts of the garden," but that he had no respect for them, and quite rightly "since one never takes walks there." His evident disdain for parterres with their detailed *broderie* points to the fact that Le Nôtre favored an overview of the whole and its parts over an emphasis on decorative details. The fact that his compositions get reduced to an admiration for nicely drawn arabesques would come only as a profound irritant to Le Nôtre.

Isolation and Lighting of the Residence

In some ways Le Nôtre seems to be a kind of hygienist before the fact; moreover, Dézallier d'Argenville uses the expression *jardins de propreté*, meaning clean or tidy gardens. Le Nôtre clearly advocates a design in which the area around the residence is largely freed of high vegetation, and surrounded only by parterres. This program was not emphatically endorsed by his contemporaries. Saint-Simon, for instance, complained in his memoirs of that "vast torrid zone" surrounding the château at Versailles.[38] Similarly, when Mademoiselle de Montpensier consulted Le Nôtre about Choisy, the latter said he would have to place all of the woods at the bottom of the site; as a result, he was dismissed and replaced by Gabriel.

The Taste for Grand Effects

At times it seems that Le Nôtre lacked realism. In any case, princely commands scarcely encouraged austere habits, as we can see in the account by Nicodemus Tessin following his visit to Versailles in 1687. Tessin describes a project for the space behind the château:

At the base of the Grande Pièce there is a mountain with a steep slope where one encounters the most fitting site for representing something grand, towards the orangery and the side of the château. Monsieur Le Nôtre showed me his design, which was admirably conceived, but which had cascades of about a hundred *aunes* [about 120 meters, or 400 feet] in width, leading one to suspect that it would not be executed, since it would take another Seine to provide the requisite water.[39]

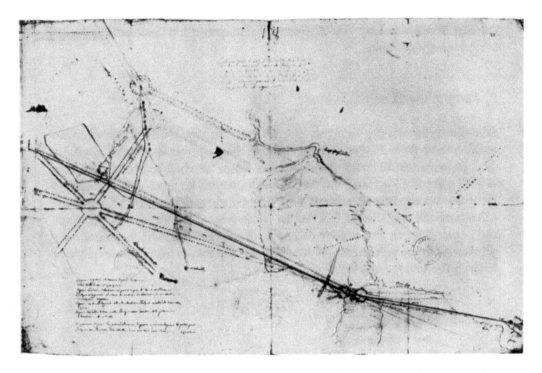

Figure 31. Le Nôtre's personal interest in laying out great infrastructures demonstrates his adherence to the perspectival sight lines of large-scale planning. Drawing by Le Nôtre for the Avenue de Picardie (Institut de France, MS. 1307, no. 74).

Speculative Projects

Le Nôtre made no attempt to isolate his gardens from the larger context. He had an extraordinary sense of the exemplary role of gardens in the organization of space, and of the necessity of connecting them to larger projects. It is well known how he employed ditches (the "ha-ha" or *saut-de-loup*), avoiding the sense of enclosure and allowing for distant views. At the château of Issy he did away with walls altogether; as a result, to borrow an expression from Dézallier d'Argenville, the garden "unites with the countryside."[40] And so the Princesse de Conti could discover the whole surrounding area in the course of a promenade, declaring: "If it is not all mine, it is all within my gaze." This opening of the garden onto space is unquestionably an affirmation of dominance. Nor should we forget that these same ordering criteria were extended to the territory as a whole—a move that, in my opinion, constitutes one of the great developments of the second half of the seventeenth century.

The plan to join the Tuileries to Saint-Germain-en-Laye is well known, and in France everyone is familiar with its partial realization. It seems that urban perspective, problems of access, and arterial infrastructure amounted to a major preoccupation for Le Nôtre. This is evident in one of the rare surviving drawings by his hand, a sketch for the Avenue de Picardie at Versailles, found among the papers of the Institut by Marguerite Charageat (Figure 31). Although such roadworks are familiar enough, there are a few surprises regarding canals in the remarks on Versailles contained in Charles Perrault's memoirs. His account not only demonstrates his familiarity with the great building projects of the time, but also reveals his participation in speculative efforts requiring energetic commercialism and international exchange. At one point serious consideration was given to the idea of joining the Loire to Versailles. While Riquet de Bonrepos and the Abbé Picard denounced the project as unfeasible from the point of view of leveling, Le Nôtre was simply captivated: ". . . what a pleasing thing it would be to see the vessels descending the river Loire with their masts and sails along the mountain [of Satory], like a glissade, and to come floating down the grand canal."[41] In this return to the ambitions of the promoters of the canal system under Henri IV, Mediterranean vessels would thus have been able to cast anchor in the Grand Canal at Versailles.

The Paradoxes of the English Garden

Earlier we noted how the exploitation of the site's limitations and the insertion into the environment were the underlying criteria for the conception of gardens in the first half of the seventeenth century. This observation compels us to reexamine the division between the naturalism of the English garden and the tyrannical rationalism of the French garden. Things are not really so simple. Although Le Nôtre is generally pigeonholed into a makeshift art historical category covering this moment of stylistic transformation, his design concepts are more in line with those of Alexander Pope, Robert Morris, or Hubert Robert.

Among the rare autograph documents by Le Nôtre, there exists in Stockholm a description of the Trianon accompanied by a colored plan. It turns out that Nicodemus Tessin, architect to the king of Sweden, had journeyed to France in 1687 precisely in order to study gardens. He has even left a description of a visit to royal parks that he made in the company of Le Nôtre. Six years later, in the hope of clarifying a few points, Tessin asked his French colleague to provide him with a textual and graphic description of the Trianon château and garden. During his visit six years earlier, when that part of the Versailles project had still been in progress, Tessin had already noted certain details:

High up, on the side of the orangery, Monsieur Le Nôtre has made a type of little marsh that he has rendered in the form of different figures, insofar as the large trees permitted it; the canals were borded with lawn, a foot deep and a bit wider; in places there were small rings (petits rondeaux) for water jets, and the slopes of the canal contained various little inclines so that the water would make noise. It was beautifully conceived, inexpensive, and an excellent way of conserving the great trees that precluded any other solution.[42]

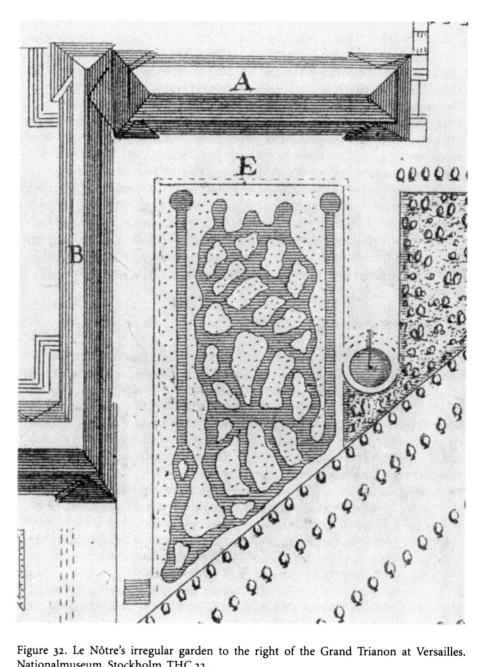

Figure 32. Le Nôtre's irregular garden to the right of the Grand Trianon at Versailles. Nationalmuseum, Stockholm, THC 22.

In his 1693 report Le Nôtre provided his own description of the place keyed to the numbers on the plan (Figure 32):

The [Bosquet des] sources runs the length of the *appartement* of galleries 10 and 11 and return from the Trianon *appartement* beneath a wood that runs along both the length and width, filled with full-grown trees that are spaced apart from each other, which provides for small canals that wind about in no particular pattern and fall into the empty spaces around the trees, with water jets placed at uneven intervals and all the canals are [both] separated and connected, flowing into each other by a very gradual slope formed by the entire wood. From both sides of the wood come twin channels falling in small waterfalls, and inside twelve-foot-high water jets, and ending in two chasms set into the ground. I cannot adequately describe to you the beauty of this place, its freshness, where the ladies go to work, play, have light meals, and [enhance] the beauty of this place. One enters it directly from the *appartements*. One walks down corner footpaths through all the different [types of] beauty, allées, bosquets, woods throughout the covered gardens. I can say that it is the only garden that I know besides the Tuileries to be so pleasing to walk in and so beautiful. I will concede the beauty and grandeur of other gardens, but this one is the most comfortable.[43]

Reading this text, which challenges a number of common assumptions, we can only wonder if the aging Le Nôtre might actually have been won over by emerging naturalist tendencies. In any case, the tendency here is toward groundedness, comfort, continuity of interior and exterior, shady areas, irregular paths, rivulets, and chasms. There is no question that this development was Le Nôtre's own, and at the very least it is amusing to have to consider him as one of the precursors of the picturesque garden. Pushing the analysis further, we could note that the interior arrangement of bosquets and the diverse spectacles already participate in that logic of the irregular—a matter of thematic continuity rather than stylistic rupture.

Moreover, returning to Vaux, we can note that Egyptomania and a taste for small garden structures are already in evidence, at least in the initial designs. If one can believe her description, Madeleine de Scudéry saw past the statue of Hercules "on both sides, fairly rough countryside and even a small rustic temple among the trees." And facing the *carré d'eaux* she saw two pyramids in imitation of the ones near Memphis, in "a fairly irregular spot of land." Citing this passage, Jean Cordey points out that they were destined to house two Egyptian sarcophagi that had been acquired by Fouquet in Marseilles and kept at Saint-Mandé.[44] They were never transported to Vaux, for reasons that we know only too well. Put up for auction, they were sold to a sculptor who then resold them to André Le Nôtre. Le Nôtre placed them in the Tuileries, near his home. After remaining in a château in Touraine during the eighteenth century, the sarcophagi found their way back to Paris, where they were installed in the Louvre museum. This anecdote demonstrates that the taste for garden structures (including temples, cenotaphs, and pyramids) was not exclusive to the eighteenth century, and that the classic garden anticipated their later role. Although there is no evidence to confirm that the Vaux structures were actually built, we should not ignore the intention.

The Treatise of Dézallier d'Argenville as Testament

The 1709 *Théorie et pratique du jardinage* by Antoine-Joseph Dézallier d'Argenville has been the object of a longstanding controversy. In the end we cannot confirm who the exact author was, or at least not the precise role of each party. As it happens, the English edition of 1728 is entitled *The theory and practice of gardening, wherein is fully handled all that relates to pleasure gardens* by le Sieur Alexandre Leblond. For a long time it was believed that the attribution to Leblond was simply a ruse by the publisher to sell more copies, since J. B. A. Leblond, an architect born in 1679, had settled abroad in 1716 after having requested a leave from the Duc d'Antin, Surintendant des Bâtiments. Leblond went on to enjoy a successful international career that took him as far as Russia, where he worked for Peter the Great.

In a work devoted to Leblond, Boris Losski concludes that there is no way of confirming that he had been Le Nôtre's pupil.[45] What we do know is that the elder Mariette published some parterre designs by Leblond that earned the admiration of the designer of Vaux. In his discussion of the book's reception, Losski recounts the testimony of the younger Mariette: "Le Blond played the greatest role in the book entitled *The theory and practice of gardening*. . . . [I]t is he who not only provided all the drawings, but also plotted out the form of the book, that was filled in under his supervision by Monsieur Désallier d'Argenville, today *maître des comptes*."[46] We know for a fact that everyone accepted the plates of the treatise as the authentic work of J. B. A. Leblond. Whatever the eventual outcome of this dispute, the book clearly has an essentially collective character and reflects the thinking of royal gardeners in the period immediately following Le Nôtre's death.

The first part of the book, divided into eight chapters, follows a structure that at first glance resembles the third book of Boyceau de la Baraudière's treatise:

1. Foreword
2. On the siting of the terrain and the use that one should make of it
3. On the general placement and distribution of gardens
4. On the different types of parterres and flower beds
5. On allées, contre-allées, and palissades
6. On woods and bosquets in general
7. On *boulingrins* and lawn enhancements (*renforcements de gazon*), as well as on large inclines, slopes, embankments, and greenswards, with the manner of laying, sowing, and maintaining them
8. On porticos, berceaux, *cabinets* of trelliswork and greenery, statues, vases, and other ornaments meant to decorate and embellish gardens

Inclines, the play of levels, and cuts into the terrain now take the place of the water and canal systems in Boyceau's treatise; otherwise, the chapters progress in like manner, even though the author claims that Boyceau and Mollet "have merely broached and, as it were, skimmed over this material." The second remark is true, the first unjust.

Most of the major themes are taken up again, such as the necessity of adapting to the site: "In order to be perfect, the placement and distribution of a general plan should conform to the situation of the land: for the greatest science of properly placing a garden is the proper knowledge and examination of the site's natural advantages and drawbacks, in order to profit from the first and correct the second; the situation is different for each garden." [47] Clearly the concern here is not to develop paradigms, but rather to conceive specific projects in terms of their constraints.

The same treatise also introduces new ideas, most notably the notion of the carefully maintained *jardin de propreté*, where "the goal is above all regularity, careful layout (*arrangement*) and that which can further flatter the view." [48] We have seen that Boyceau neither praises the utilitarian garden (as Olivier de Serres had done) nor dismisses the effects that can be obtained from it. But now the split is expressly acknowledged: "All of those kitchen gardens, all of those orchards, beautiful as they may be, are always placed in areas remote and separate from other gardens: clear proof that they are considered more necessary for the utility of a house than for enhancing its beauty and magnificence."

Chapter 3, which deals with the general layout of gardens, seems to us the most important, since the author's recommendations are clearly drawn directly from Le Nôtre. Simply trotted out with no apparent coherence, these remarks are more like a collection of maxims, gleaned over the course of conversations or visits to work sites, than a chapter expounding a methodology. The formulas contained here might treat general problems just as easily as rules of proportion or the arrangement of details. They are typical of the basic knowledge that an old master instills in his disciples: a series of assertions, given without justification and revealing an extensive savoir-faire. As compared with Boyceau la Baraudière, the tone is much more dogmatic, and more thoroughly entrenched in experience than in any kind of strictly theoretical program.

Still, disjointed as they may be, the following essential precepts constitute a basic corpus of knowledge about the composition of French gardens:

Above all, seek to create a pleasing whole rather than be too noticeable.

It is better to be content with a reasonable expanse that is well-cultivated, than to have those vast parks, three quarters of which are usually neglected.

One can establish four fundamental maxims for the proper layout of a garden: first, to make art give way to nature; second, to avoid making a garden too gloomy; third, not to disclose (*découvrir*) too much; and fourth, to make it appear larger than it really is.

Variety is necessary not only for the general design of a garden, but also in each separate component, since it would be disagreeable to find the same design on both sides. . . . [O]ne should not repeat the same components on both sides except in exposed areas where the eye can compare them with each other and judge their conformity.

In one's designs one should avoid petty little mannerisms, and always work in a beautiful and grand manner.

The general proportions of gardens of average size are to be a third (or even a half) greater in length than width, so that the parts become oblong and more graceful to the eye.

One should always descend from the building into the garden by way of a stairway with at least three steps; this keeps the building drier and healthier.

The first thing one should see is the parterre, which should occupy the areas closest to the building. The choice of parterres should be considered a small matter in comparison with the general arrangement and apportionment of gardens.

When adopted without recourse to the morphology of the site (even though this had been the prime motivating factor of seventeenth-century garden design), these formulas constituted the common basis of all neoclassical productions, which can only be described as reductive.

Parks, Forests, and Planning

4

THE *SURINTENDANCE DES BÂTIMENTS DU ROI*

The Role of Colbert

Surprising as it may seem, the man who was effectively the main coordinator of garden projects was Jean-Baptiste Colbert (1619–83). He made the important decisions in this and all areas concerning the organization of the realm, and he took a special interest in his role as the director of the Bâtiments du Roi, or royal building administration. In his memoirs Charles Perrault maintains that Colbert began preparing for this position long before it was conferred on him:

As early as the end of 1662, when Monsieur Colbert had predicted or knew already that the king would make him Surintendant des Bâtiments, he began to prepare for carrying out this duty, which he considered much more important than it appeared to be in the hands of Monsieur de Ratabon.[1]

Perrault also recounts an interesting anecdote regarding the opening and frequenting of gardens. Following the replanting of the Tuileries gardens, Colbert had envisaged closing them to the public in order to keep them from being damaged. Perrault's description of his own plea to keep the gardens open indicates the temper of the time:

When he had reached the *grand allée*, I said to him: "You would not believe, Monsieur, the respect which everyone, down to the most insignificant *bourgeois*, has for this garden. Not only do the women and small children never take it into their heads to pick any flowers, but they do not even touch them; they walk here as if they were all very reasonable people. The gardeners, Monsieur, can bear witness to this. It would be a public affliction not to be able to come here to walk about, especially now that no one may enter the Luxembourg Gardens or the Hôtel de Guise." "It is only idlers who come here," he said to me. "People come here," I replied, "who are recovering from illness, to take the air; they come here to talk about business, about marriages, and about everything which is dealt with more appropriately in a garden than in a church, where in future people would have to meet . . ." He smiled at this speech, and since meanwhile most of the Tuileries gardeners had presented themselves before him, he asked them if the public did not wreak havoc in their garden. "Not at all, Monseigneur," they replied, almost in chorus. . . . Monsieur Colbert made a tour of the garden, gave his orders, and said not a word about closing the entrance to anyone at all.[2]

The Surintendance des Bâtiments du Roi could be defined as a kind of Ministry of Culture, since it simultaneously encompassed royal châteaux, public monuments, gardens, arts, academies, and royal manufactures. Colbert clearly sensed the economic impact of this area of activity, whose considerable development he undertook to direct and manage. His letters, instructions and memoirs, collected by Pierre Clément in 1867, bear witness to this. He oversaw this administration down to the last detail, while relying on the academy of architecture that he established as a type of consultative body.

Colbert's orders and regulations for the buildings of Versailles, drawn up at Saint-Germain on October 24, 1674,[3] give us a very precise idea of the extent of his intervention. This document apparently appoints a certain Lefèvre as overseer of the park property, charged with ensuring that the contractors employ the number of workers specified in the estimate: "make a count of Colinet's boys, ensure that he always has as many as he said he would, and send me his confirmation of this each month." The same advice is given for work on the canal, for the maintenance of the mill, and for the verification of the pumps, where he is to ensure "that they lack nothing and always have a double provision of all shafts, wood, and screws for every tool." And for the fountains as well, Colbert insists on frequent visits, verification of manpower, and prompt repairs. His advice even extends to details, as when he decides "to recommend chandeliers for the grotto," to complete the marble bases and statues, or to end the allées at a given point.

Colbert paid such close attention to the form and execution of the smallest details that he can be considered the project's executive architect. His use of technical language indicates a specialized knowledge extending to such matters as the manufacturing of drystone drains, substituting sand for rich soil, paving basins, or establishing the correct site and slope for canals.

Le Nôtre is mentioned only once in the entire enumeration, in relation to the planting of allées: "Complete all of the allées around the canal, according to the agreement made with Marin. As soon as it is time for planting, have Ballon do it immediately, following the report by Sieur Le Nostre." Le Nôtre is thus responsible for the conception, but in this case not for the execution or coordination of the various works, a fact that significantly alters the prevailing image of his role. Even more surprising is the fact that the celebrated minister had also been a kind of general garden inspector.

In addition to the treasurers working under Colbert, there were three Intendants et Ordonnateurs des Bâtiments and three Contrôleurs Généraux. The treasurers, intendants, and contrôleurs were described as "alternating," since they carried out their duties for one year out of every three. Immediately below these top-level administrators, the payrolls record a certain number of officers, such as the First Architect and First Painter, whose duties extended to all of the royal houses. Below the artists one finds the personnel of the various houses, and finally the contractors.

The Various Personnel in Gardening

As early as 1664, the royal accounts list the king's gardeners at Versailles as Laurent Périer, Marin, Trumel, Henry Dupuis, and Macé Fourché. All five gardeners figure in payments for supplies, or for laying out a particular parterre or allée. Although titled, these gardeners were halfway between high officials and ordinary contractors, and were paid by the job.[4] We also find mention of a certain Pierre Picq, flower supplier, and in 1665 of Mathieu Macon planting fruit trees in the kitchen garden, as well as Pierre Desgots who supplied orange trees. In 1666 the same Pierre Desgots is mentioned in the Louvre accounts for having pruned the elms in the Allée du Mail, as well as Claude Carbonnel whose workers had installed parterres.

There is also mention of the *rocailleur* Jean Delaunay working in the grotto, and Denis Jolly, who installed hydraulic organs. In addition we read of Simon Bouchard, and then of his wife Françoise (Le Nôtre's sister), who succeeded her husband after his death. Around 1670 one finds mention of Le Bouteux, who was especially involved at the Trianon. In the chapter devoted to the corporation of gardeners we saw that the Bouteux family had been in the trade for generations.

The aligning of the allées of the Grand Parterre was carried out in 1668 by another specialist, Guillaume Le Breton. Also mentioned is a certain Henry, whose job was to find plants and flowers for the royal houses. The planting of avenues constitutes a separate task, for which Ballon was reimbursed in 1669 "for the expenses that he incurred with three gardeners whom he had brought from Flanders in order to select, uproot and move the elms and linden trees that had been purchased by the king."[5] We should note that in addition to the enormous number of small plants that were brought in at the time for the great park, there are references to the planting of more mature specimens: "To the Sieur des Leslées, Receiver General of Finances for Artois, for his reimbursement of the sums that he spent on the purchase and transport of 11,238 trees that he had purchased in Flanders and had sent to Versailles, 13,980 *livres*."[6] Also in 1669 we find mention of the demolition of the Trianon church by a certain Mazereau, in addition to records relating to the transport and payment of boats destined for the Grand Canal, such as the galliot designed by the engineer Le Roy, which alone cost 11,955 *livres*.[7]

The number of gardening suppliers and employees increased over the years. In 1671 we find Michel Dubois, Louis Barbier, Antoine Deslauriers, Jean Frade, Jean Bille, Antoine de Mollet, Claude Guyot, Claude Jacques, and Jacques Vautier. It was customary in this century for specialized professions to be maintained within the same family. So it was for the mole-catchers Jacques, André, and Martin Liard, who received 476 *livres* for having caught 2,723 of the creatures in 1665 at Fontainebleau, Saint-Germain, and Versailles.

We find similar family monopolies among the fountaineers, such as the Jolly, Denis, and (in particular) Francini families. The Florentine Tomasso Francini had moved to France in 1599.[8] He was initially charged with the care of the waters and fountains at Fontainebleau, and in 1623 Louis XIII granted letters patent making him Intendant Général of the Waters and Fountains of France. François Francini (1617–88), his son, succeeded his father at the age of twenty; in 1642 he was named Commissioner General of Wars in Normandy before going on to become a royal councilor and maître d'hôtel, a lawyer in the Parlement, a Criminal Lieutenant of the Short Robe, Provost, and Viscount of Paris. Indeed, he was simultaneously Prefect of Police and head fountaineer. This rapid and surprising ascent also reminds us that Le Nôtre was not alone in winning honors, and that some very enviable successes practically eclipsed his own, at least in terms of immediate renown. Historians have not always properly understood this situation.

The gardens also included the Fruictier du Roy, or royal orchard, managed by Jean de La Quintinie. Nicodemus Tessin reports that during the appropriate season he delivered close to 150 melons and 4,000 figs each day for the use of the court.[9] Thirty valet gardeners were employed in this intensive production.

Comparison of Revenues

Indexing of revenues was unknown in the seventeenth century. Aside from promotions or appointments to new posts, the officers of the king's household were paid on the same basis for twenty years and more. This can be verified for the period around 1664. For his own role as chief executive, Colbert granted himself 15,000 *livres*, but it was the painter Charles Le Brun who received the top salary of 20,800 *livres*, whereas the treasurers Le Ménestral and Le Buègue received only 2,800. Architects' appointments varied greatly. They ranged from 6,000 *livres* for Le Vau to 1,200 *livres* for André Félibien and 1,000 *livres* for Pierre Le Muet, Libéral Bruant, Antoine Le Pautre, and Daniel Gittard, with only 500 *livres* each for the year 1675, which probably indicates no more than extended leaves by architects who also had a large private clientele.

The same disparities are found among gardeners, although we must keep in mind that payments included both a salary and contracting fees. Macé Fourché, who took care of the Petit Parc at Versailles, received 6,000 *livres*; Marin Trumel, keeper of the orangerie and the flower garden, received 3,000 *livres*; and Masson, in charge of the kitchen garden, received 1,500. Charles Mollet was given 500 *livres* for parterre designs, plus 1,000 *livres* in total. The younger Denis, fountaineer at Versailles, was paid 7,900 *livres* for his services. Jean de La Quintinie received 2,000 *livres* in appointments plus 2,000 in gratuities, whereas Le Bouteux, in charge of the Trianon, was allotted 17,500 *livres* in 1673, which is more than the combined wages of Colinet, Trumel, and Vautier (14,800 *livres* in the same year).

André Le Nôtre's revenues were divided up as follows: 5,440 *livres* for his roles as Contrôleur Général of the buildings, gardens, arts and manufactures of France, to which were added 1,200 *livres* for parterre designs, and 3,000 *livres* for the care of the new Grand Parterre at the Tuileries. This amounts to an annual total of 9,640 *livres*, occasionally increased by bonus payments for extreme diligence or for extra work demanded by certain projects. In 1670, for example, he received an additional 4,000 *livres*.

Precise Duties of Le Nôtre

Among the royal building accounts for the year 1670, we find at Val-de-Grâce a payment of 5,000 *livres* to the contractors Leduc and Duval "which includes all the additions they have made to the buildings of the said abbey following the estimate made by André Le Nostre and the prior of Monbehon." [10] Le Nôtre must have been competent in architecture if he was in a position to verify invoices and certify work in this domain. Clearly his field of activity was not limited to gardens.

Outside of his duties as Contrôleur Général des Bâtiments, which required him to handle a variety of problems, Le Nôtre provided the overall designs and general layout of ground plans. Yet in addition to these conceptual responsibilities, he continued to work on certain projects at the same level and with the same duties as the regular gardeners. The terms of such an agreement are found in the accounts of 1671:

To André Le Nostre, who has been assigned the maintenance of the newly planted parterres facing the Tuileries palace, for his wages regarding the said maintenance, consisting of cleaning, packing down, and raking the great terrace facing the said palace, the central Grande Allée, the contre-allées, the circumference and grounds of the large Rondeau, along with the palisades and the crescent containing pine, yew, and cyprus trees up to the first horse chestnut tree at the central Grande Allée, and the transverse allée planted with trees enclosing the square that contained the pond, the allée of elms at the end of the parterres where the rondeau is, terminating on the right with the Allée du Mail, and on the left at the grand terrace to the side of the river; against [the property of] Monsieur de Congis, eight squares of *parterres en broderie* which are to be clipped and tidied throughout, along with the *plates-bandes* and transverse allées and the area around the basins. Will oversee the digging and manuring of the young plantings of the said parterre, and will fill them each season with flowers of the same variety as those currently found there, which he is to raise, replant, and replenish at his own expense – 3000 *livres*.[11]

Here Le Nôtre is paid as a service provider rather than a high official of the royal administration. His style of living was certainly honorable, with a household including two gardeners, a cook, a chambermaid, a lackey, and a coachman. His art collection included works by Claude Lorrain, Nicolas Poussin, Rembrandt, and Bruegel, as well as a collection of prints that ran to twenty-four volumes. In *A Journey to Paris in the Year 1698*, Martin Lister notes that

Monsieur *le Nostre*'s Cabinet, or Rooms, wherein he keeps his fine things, the Controller of the Kings Gardens, at the side of the *Tuilleries*, was worth seeing. . . . There were in the three Appartments, into which it is divided, (the uppermost of which is an Octogon Room with a *Dome*) a great Collection of choice Pictures, Porcellans . . .some old *Roman* Heads and

Busto's, and intire Statues; a great Collection of *Stamps* very richly bound up in Books. . . .
[H]e had a great Collection of Medals in four Cabinets. . . . In this Cabinet I saw many very
rare old China Vessels.[12]

The curiosity cabinet was a fashion imported from Italy, where it had apparently
been started by Giambattista della Porta. To assemble such a cabinet during the
seventeenth century was to place oneself among the most accomplished minds of
the day. More than a sign of social status, such collecting demonstrated an interest
in technology and the history of civilizations. Although the thirst for knowledge
expressed in the assembly of such collections might seem untidy by more recent
standards, it did lay the foundations of modern scientific practices by establishing
of the kinds of classifications and taxonomies later studied by Michel Foucault.

Already in his lifetime Le Nôtre enjoyed an international reputation. We can
gauge his importance from the account by Père Desmolets of his 1678 visit to Italy:
"Bernini wanted to meet Le Nôtre. The latter, when paying him a visit, was pleas-
antly surprised to find on the great man's desk the collection of prints depicting
some of his works. Bernini told him he did not know who the author was, but that
they partook of a rare genius." Even "Pope Innocent, who was still living, having
learned from Monsieur the Duc d'Estrées, ambassador of France, that Le Nôtre was
in Rome, wished to see him, and granted him a fairly long audience . . . after the
genuflections the pope had him rise and asked to see the plans of Versailles that he
had heard so much about." [13]

To complete this celebrity, Le Nôtre was ennobled in 1675 and decorated with
the Cross of Saint Michael. His retirement was motivated partly by his advanced
age, but also largely because of the radical difference in conception that was forming between him and the king. The excesses of Marly are abundantly described in
Saint-Simon: the planting of full-grown trees, clearings replacing deep woods
within a matter of months, incessant changes in the organization of a given space.
This manner of violating nature had probably reached a stage at which Le Nôtre
could no longer bring himself to play along:

Although Louis XIV did not cease to admire the rare genius of Le Nôtre in the area of gardening, the great prince was eager to see other geniuses emerge, whose acceptance would be
due only to him. Le Nôtre was now eighty years old. His long exposure to the court had not
diminished his love for the truth: he did not find that the greatest king in the world understood the art of gardening as perfectly as he did, and he said so in no uncertain terms.[14]

REGIONAL-SCALE PLANNING AT VERSAILLES

The Versailles project is inseparable from the general policies implemented by
Colbert. It was part of a large-scale attempt at economic redeployment, based
on a desire to transform the deep structures of French society. By the time of
Louis XIV's accession, the lack of commercial organization had reached crisis level.

The nobility was at fault, since in comparison to England they had been reluctant to turn to merchant activities. This was not for want of incentive, since as early as 1462 an edict of Louis XI had opened up commerce to nobles, regardless of their standing. *Dérogeance* (the loss of noble status) had been reinstituted in the sixteenth century, but it was practiced only in the coastal provinces. The creation of two India companies by Colbert continued this process by offering the aristocracy the opportunity to invest without loss of rank. A number of edicts encouraged maritime commerce, naval construction, and armament. The importance of water at Versailles, and the presence of miniature ships made expressly for the Grand Canal, are merely the symbolic counterpart and summation of a much larger policy—and the same man led the way in both of these enterprises.

Cartography

The reign of Louis XIV saw the emergence of an entire movement toward the establishment of what we might, in retrospect, call a state-centered human geography relying on maps and statistics. The origin of this organizational urge should certainly be sought in Jesuit teaching and in their ethnological experience, discussed above. The first steps seem to have been taken by the *surintendant* d'Effiat (owner of the château of Chilly), who sent his provincial *intendants* a set of instructions that Colbert reinstituted in 1664 in a document recommending the establishment of good maps showing administrative divisions. He noted that these maps should be accompanied by information about such matters as bishoprics and abbeys (including their revenues and their wealth); the organization of legal institutions and the nobility; finances and tax collecting mechanisms; principal resources and local activities; and aspects of rivers, including their navigational possibilities. As curious as it might seem, the Versailles project and its extension into the southwestern region of Paris played a decisive role in this process, insofar as it was the testing ground for cartographic and surveying techniques that led to a global conception of national territory.

After 1664, and throughout the entire reign of Louis XIV, the Académie des Sciences was instructed to supply the most precise possible image of the country. The first act of scientific cartography was the Abbé Picard's measuring of a meridian arc between Amiens and la Ferté-Alais, using a chain of thirteen triangles. As the base or reference measurement he used the straight road of 5,663 *toises* joining Villejuif and Juvisy. This still exists today in the form of the Nationale 7 highway, where a pyramid has been erected at one of the Juvisy crossroads to commemorate its establishment. This sector of the Paris region, already distinguished by residential density, now found itself at the head of an operation that anticipated development on a territorial scale.

It is largely around 1670 that the royal building accounts reveal expenses relating to cartographic projects:

On June 11, 1670, to Meissieurs Niquet, Vivier, Pivet, and Dupuy, in payment for geographic maps that they have made of the *généralité* of Paris and other provinces of the realm: 3,000 *livres*. . . . To Sieur Cassini, mathematician, 6,000 *livres* for his ordinary appointments and 3,000 additional gratuity for the present year. . . . To Sieur Riquet de Bonrepos, in 1671, an advance of 125,000 *livres* on 3,600,000. . . . On August 27 of this same year, to Sieur Picard, mathematician, for the cost of travel relating to a number of astronomical observations, 1,000 *livres*.[15]

Here we can see that the completion of maps (a nationwide concern) was financed by the treasury of the royal building accounts and was strictly linked with planning projects bearing no relation to the royal residences. On this point, we have already cited the 1678 accounts remunerating the gardener Thierry for simultaneously plotting routes in the Versailles region and drawing up maps.

Around 1679 the Marly project appears in the accounts, and in 1681 one finds road workers, laborers, and gardeners working on the avenues of Marly, Louveciennes, La Selle, Rocquencourt, Clagny, and Glatigny. The final stage of the diffusion and extension of parks into outside areas, these avenues clearly point to the notion of regional-scale planning, with Versailles at the epicenter—a system perfectly illustrated in Cassini's hunting map. The revival of road building was an urgent matter at the time, since the annual budget for public works, which had reached around 3,600,000 livres in 1608, had fallen below 100,000 livres before the arrival of Colbert.

Surveying and Water Conveyance

Cartography and surveying techniques developed in tandem: here, too, royal gardens played a preponderant role. The digging of the Grand Canal of Versailles, in particular, could not have been realized without the arbitration of the Académie des Sciences. This is evident from the following anecdote related by Charles Perrault in his *Parallèle des Anciens et des Modernes*:

When the Grand Canal of Versailles was decided on, orders were given to the workers laboring on the site, masons and fountaineers, to survey the terrain where it was to be situated. They all found, using their ordinary levels and in the old manner, that the terrain sloped down ten feet between the edge of the Petit Parc, where the canal was to begin, and the place where it was to end. Members of the Académie were called in, and with their levels they found a slope of only two feet where ten had been found. The canal was built on the basis of this measurement, and when the water was placed in it, it turned out that they had only been off by an inch.[16]

We should note that on this occasion the academicians made use of a completely new apparatus fitted with a telescope and an adjustable surveying rod.

The academicians also intervened after the Sieur de Bonrepos, who designed the Canal des Deux Mers, proposed to the king that the Loire be linked to Versailles. We know that this proposition had been one of Le Nôtre's great dreams. But

Figure 33. The Grand Canal at Versailles, which Le Nôtre believed could have served as a place for mooring Mediterranean vessels arriving through a system of adjoining canals. Print by Gabriel Pérelle.

alas, when the Abbé Picard was called in for a second opinion, he used precise measurements to prove the operation untenable. The whole process was nonetheless necessary, and the fact remains that, alongside this attempt, canalization and the straightening of river beds were pressing concerns, serving as they did to facilitate commercial exchange. Colbert had numerous waterways improved and opened to navigation, and he established a number of communications routes, including the canal between Saint-Omer and Calais and the one from the Loire to the Loing. He also dreamed of joining the Somme and the Oise, and asked Riquet de Bonrepos to consider the junction of the Saône and the Seine, a project that later resulted in the canals of Charolais and Bourgogne.

Technological Advances

In terms of water supply, the establishment of the Versailles park was an unprecedented achievement. During his interview with the pope, Le Nôtre had shown him the Versailles plans. Père Desmolets recounts that "His Holiness was astonished by the quantity of canals, fountains, water jets, and cascades, and believed that a river provided the prodigious abundance of water, but his surprise redoubled when he was told that there wasn't one, that an infinite number of ponds had been made and the water was channeled into huge reservoirs by means of conduits and pipes."[17]

Moving beyond the usual criticism of the pointless extravagance of the Versailles waters, we should view them first and foremost as a technological testing ground that gave rise to enormous progress in plumbing and water conveyance within the space of a few years.

Denis's plan of the Versailles canalization is the very image of this innovation in public works. The pipe networks were planned and designed in tandem with the general layout, just as today one might plan a city or neighborhood. Here, too, the garden anticipates the modern urban project. Water circulation systems came very late to long-established cities, where they had to contend with the inconvenience of existing substructures. Yet at Versailles they were conceived in all their complexity from the very beginning, with the scientific academicians perfecting new mechanisms and solving the problems of regulating pressure, pipe size, and rate of flow over enormous distances.

The year 1672 was important for the completion of infrastructures.[18] The accounts anticipate the following expenses:

3,300 *livres* for moving earth for the Grande Avenue of Versailles and for planting trees there

264,000 *livres* for digging the Grand Canal, masonry, and transport

60,000 *livres* for bringing water from the Bonnières pond and drilling through the mountain

40,000 *livres* for completing the windmills on the mountain

40,000 *livres* to make the water reach the reservoir at the top of the park

14,000 *livres* to complete the reservoir to receive the water from the windmills

100,000 *livres* for the lead pipes at Versailles

100,000 *livres* for the iron pipes

40,000 *livres* for taps and other fittings

These three final headings, which might seem banal, are actually extremely important, since that same year led to an important technological breakthrough in the form of preassembled iron pipes. Previous to the Versailles experiment, methods of pipe manufacture had been rather random; some pipes were made of tree trunks laid end to end and joined with rings that disintegrated very quickly; others were made of breakable terra-cotta, and still others of lead with joints that could scarcely withstand high pressure. The canalization of gardens was therefore an unsatisfactory process until the adoption of iron pipes solved most of the problems involved. The afterlife of this solution is familiar enough. In any case, beginning around 1673,[19] only iron pipes are mentioned in the building accounts.

The history of the Académie Royale des Sciences[20] recounts the details of this

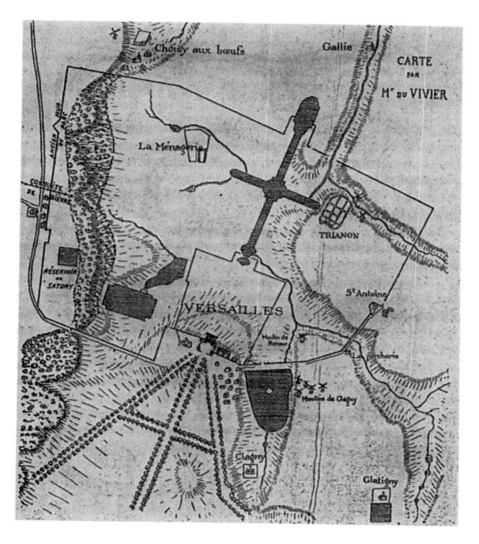

Figure 34. Intermediate state of hydraulic installations at Versailles, before the suppression of the Etang de Clagny.

evolution and the progress that enabled the royal building administration to produce

the waters of Versailles, whose beauty was an entirely new spectacle in the world, and which became more surprising with each passing day, having made fashionable the science of water and mathematics (uncouth though they might have seemed), demonstrating their utility for the pleasure and magnificence of a great king. Water jets need help from geometry, and as the academy often deals with this subject, Monsieur Roemer provided a universal rule with which to judge the value of all the machines used to raise water by horsepower. . . . Monsieur

Mariotte went into much greater detail regarding the expenditure involved in water jets, and the amount [of water] necessary to run them. This depends on the relative speed of flow, on the size of the fittings through which [the waters] emerge, and the relative amount of friction in the conduit pipes: all circumstances which geometry alone can evaluate. . . . [T]here is no issue, down to the thickness of the metal used for pipes, that should not be settled by geometry.

The evolution of the general system of water provision in the Versailles park, with respect to the extent of the project, also gave rise to numerous advances. At first the only source had been the Clagny pond, from which the water was drawn by six pumps and three windmills. In 1670 the Trianon gardens demanded a new increase in output, as the pond threatened to dry up. The problem was averted by the establishment of a recycling system. Having run their course toward the lowest portions of the garden, the waters were directed back to the pond by means of a pump and a windmill called a return mill (*moulin de retour*), a system not unlike the ones used in modern-day water purification stations.

The increasing demand for water led to a definitive solution, equally indebted to the Abbé Picard's observations. Surface waters were now drained from all of the surrounding plateaus through a 180-kilometer network of channels, ponds, and aqueducts stretching between Versailles, Saclay, and Rambouillet, with a total draining surface of fifteen thousand hectares. So not only was the modern technique of forced water pipes instigated at Versailles, but also that of basins to collect rain water. Supplying the park's 1400 water jets entailed redeveloping the entire region. Moreover, the drinkable water issuing from the springs of Chesnay, Rocquencourt, and the forest of Marly did not use the same network as the waters destined for hydraulic installations. This double-circuit system would later be revived by Baron Haussmann in his large-scale renovations of Paris.

REGULATION OF SPACE

Architecture, Garden, Park, and Territory

Clearly our whole way of organizing space is inherited from the classic parks, either by directly importing entire models (cities, gardens) or, more often, through specific elements (star-shaped crossings, avenues, fountain basins, the monumental axiality of compositions, perspective effects, etc.). In some cases, new settlements have even successfully reused classic road networks that are still clearly visible, as at Sainte-Geneviève-des-Bois, Juvisy, and Maisons-Laffitte. More insidiously, on the level of spatial conceptions and their systems of relations, the classic garden sets the stage for modern methods of urbanization and contemporary planning. Parks have clearly played an instigative role in the hierarchization, qualification, and quantification of space.

We have already seen that seventeenth-century garden design is not a simple matter of aesthetics. The principles of adaptation to the site, the types of layout, and the internal organization all lead to new potential in the exploitation of soil and management of resources. Gardens are far more innovative, in every respect, than contemporaneous urban schemas like the town of Richelieu. There the uniform grid simply generates neutral, non-polarized spaces, really no more than islands except for the square and the main road.

The garden and the forest both underwent an unprecedented development in the seventeenth century, when they became the focus of new theories and regulations. The rapid organization of gardens had a major impact on the structure of forests. We can witness the spread of a system of distribution that began in architecture and moved into the horticultural domain, then on to the park, to the forest, and eventually to a territorial and urban level.

In his 1623 architectural treatise[21] Pierre Le Muet already notes the necessity of the proper relations of rooms; the distribution of *appartements* undergoes a veritable revolution over the course of the seventeenth and eighteenth centuries. In a recent work, Jean-Marie Pérouse de Montclos establishes the genealogy of this transformation of seigneurial living spaces, and demonstrates that it is a peculiarly French phenomenon.[22] The seigneurial residence of the early seventeenth century is essentially composed of multi-purpose rooms extending the entire width of the building, whereas beginning in the second half of the century the parts begin to specialize and multiply in response to various functions. Hence we witness the appearance of bedrooms, antichambers, cabinets, wardrobes, galleries, and even winter and summer dining rooms.

This process of increasing enrichment and complexity can also be observed in the organization of gardens, which copy forms and borrow terms from the plans of living quarters, as evident in the following description by Boyceau de la Baraudière:

Elevated structures also have great grace in gardens, and provide great relief by their covers and shadows; they mark and partition off spaces. They are formed by allées or galleries, covered with trees or made into berceaux or *plats-fonds*, with carpentry or wooden rods that the foliage covers over. Rooms, chambers, and cabinets with their suites are thus formed, covered in domes or crowns, in the form of *corps de logis* and pavilions.[23]

As the distinctions among rooms and their uses become manifest, the exterior spaces also branch off and become specialized. We can sense a great difference between the writings of Boyceau de la Baraudière and those of Dézallier d'Argenville in the following century:

All of the different types of parterres can be reduced to the following four types: *parterres de broderie, parterres de compartiment, parterres a l'anglaise,* and cut-out parterres (*ceux de pièces coupées*) . . . woods and bosquets provide relief in gardens. . . . As for their forms and designs, they can espouse different manners. . . . [T]he most ordinary form is the star, the intersection or the cross of Saint Andrew, and the *patte d'oie*; yet one can also make cloisters, labyrinths, quincunxes, lawns, rooms (*salles*), cabinets, chains (*chapelets*), checkerboards, crossroads, culs-de-poêle, culs-de-sac, theaters and ballrooms, covered rooms, natural and artificial berceaux, fountains, islands, cascades, and stretches of water or greenery.[24]

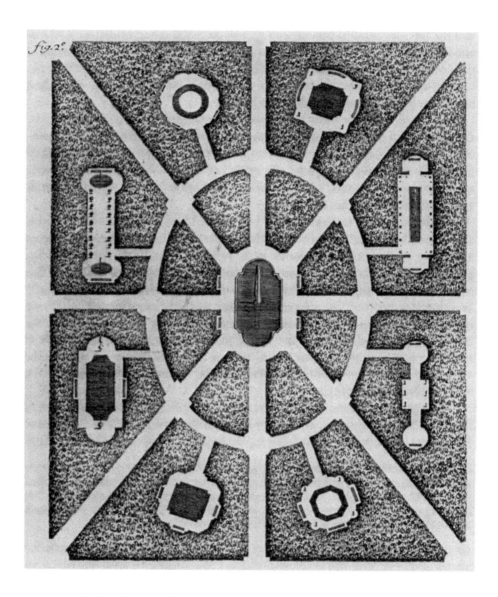

Figure 35. The distribution of *appartements* served as the organizational model for gardens, as in this arrangement of *cabinets de verdure* taken from Dézallier d'Argenville, *La théorie et la pratique du jardinage* (1747). At a later stage the garden would export its organizational logic to the forest, and then to the territory as a whole.

Between the parterre and the deep forest a type of crescendo is orchestrated, with the park acting as a transitional space:

There are several types of woods that can be reduced to the following six types: forests and large high woods, copses (*les bois taillis*), medium-sized bosquets with high palissades, exposed and compartmentalized bosquets, bosquets planted in quincunx, and young trees.[25]

Parks and large-scale gardens are the first examples of outdoor spaces created from plans involving criteria of hierarchization and linkage based on an extremely diverse operational vocabulary expressing an architectural logic. Zoning principles, based on criteria of opposition and exclusion, are also very much in evidence:

In placing and distributing the different parts of the garden, one must always take care to set them one against the other; for example a wood should be placed beside a parterre and not a lawn beside a basin, which would be a void against a void—something that must always be avoided by placing solid against void and flat against relief to create opposition.[26]

Clearly modern urbanism's planar masses are determined not only by the organizational criteria of life under economic industrialism, but also by attitudes developed in the seventeenth century.

Garden theory also plays a part, though to a lesser extent than forest legislation, in developing the foundations of regulated urbanism. For instance one does find rules relating to proportion and prospect. According to Boyceau de la Baraudière, "the width of allées should be proportionate to their length and to the height of the borders or palissades (these latter should not surpass two-thirds of the width)."[27]

A process of interrelated regulation is instigated and sustained throughout the entire composition:

the *grandes allées*, lined with espaliers or high borders that block one's view of the garden, should be accompanied by contre-allées, of half their size or a bit less, so as to serve as an exposed walkway and to serve the surrounding garden spaces; these [contre-allées] should also determine the proportions of other crossroads that run into them or reveal the surrounding spaces.[28]

Hierarchy of values, proportional relationships among the elements, spaces that serve and are served: classic garden theory establishes rules of composition that will ultimately be perpetuated by the future Ecole des Beaux-Arts.

The Reorganization of Forests: Origins of Zoning and Urban Planning

The forest was the object of the first great reorganization of physical space undertaken by the state under Colbert. Idle and indistinct places came to haunt the late seventeenth-century mind, leading to the corrective planning measures of the great

Figure 36. The Versailles Salle de Bal. Print by Gabriel Pérelle.

forest reformation. These transformations originated in a horticultural conception of productive space.

In the medieval economy, and in that of the sixteenth century, wood was one of the most important raw materials available, and the forest usefully extended agricultural space through a whole series of user's rights. In addition to pasturage, gathering, acorn harvesting, and the provision of lumber and deadwood, an entire world of small tradesmen such as charcoal burners, lumberjacks, and tree planters earned a living from the forest.

A corollary of the demographic surge and the growth of villages in the early sixteenth century was the extension of clearings, a process exacerbated by the armies with their heedless use of wood, as well as by the financial situation of seigneurs, ecclesiastics, and even royalty, who profited from the significant clearing and sale of land.

Because of the economic ramifications, those in power reserved the right to keep an eye on forest property by means of *réformations*, which were regular inspections carried out by specialized officers. In the seventeenth century, the situation was no better than in the sixteenth, and these *réformations* ceased almost entirely after 1635. Before 1661 there was no overall image of the royal forests, and no way of knowing their exact size.[29] In this context, Colbert's decree of 1669 represents an unprecedented regulatory standard. And yet the issues had already been raised by two important works: *Instruction sur le fait des eaux et forêts* (*Instruction on the matter of waters and forests*, 1603) by Jacques de Chauffourt, and *Les edits et ordonnances des rois* (*The edicts and decrees of kings*, 1610) by Sainctyon, a type of critical compilation concerning previous legislation.

The royal building accounts (and especially those of 1664–65) enable us to gauge, alongside the exterior planning of the royal residences, this general move toward forest development and organization. The most important campaign took place in 1664, in the vicinities of Saint-Germain-en-Laye and Vésinet. That year Jean La Lande, Laurent Estienne, Nicolas Morsan, Jean de Reynie, and Thomas Vitry were paid for planting a total of 5,401,800 tree shoots. This amounts to the creation of an entire forest in the extension of the Saint-Germain park.

The term *aménagement* (planning, development, management), which originally pertained to silviculture, embraces a certain number of operations that consist in regulating the method of cultivating and exploiting forest plantings over a period of one or several cycles. The process begins with the establishment of two general types of statistics. On the one hand, a map of the forest is drawn up, indicating contours, relief, roads, and rivers. On the other hand, one determines factors such as plant species, overall condition, the number of clearings, and finally the parceling or division of land on the basis of plantings, age, and quality. The next stage involves determining the system of exploitation, the felling rotation, and so on. A consideration of these methods clearly reveals the extent to which economic statistics and urban studies are indebted to forestry analysis.

The initial sense of the term *aménagement* did not originate with Jacques de Chauffort or Sainctyon. It seems to make its first appearance in Article XVII of the Ordonnance des Eaux et Forêts of August 1669:

They [the Grands Maîtres des Eaux et Forêts] will send every year to our council, directly to the comptroller general of our finances, three statements of sales made by them. The first will contain the quantity of wood sold in each maîtrise [i.e. each master's jurisdiction]; the second will contain the sums which they have levied on officers of particular maîtrises . . . and the third the sums that they have set for sowing and replanting empty areas, and clearing dead and stunted woods, in order to bring them back to standard, and for making ditches and other extra expenses and costs normally incurred in maintenance [*aménagement*] of our forests.[30]

The entire text of the Ordonnance reveals a relentlessly meddling attitude toward private property: the Grands Maîtres may, at their leisure, make inspections of the woods and forests belonging to the Church, the communities, and in mortmain.[31]

Even the method of cutting and direction of felling become objects of precise recommendations. National objectives severely curtailed the latitude given to proprietors.

The forest is described in the way one would a city. It is divided into cantons,[32] determined by *layes* (sections of forest) or paths traced by the surveyors. The corners of each sector are marked with trees called *pieds-corniers*, a term borrowed from carpentry. These *pieds-corniers* are connected by lines of trees called *lisières* (skirts or borders) that give form to the alignments, while the areas of foliage constituting a kind of façade along the limits of each sector are called *parois* (walls).[33] These terms are clearly drawn from architecture, and the method of description could just as easily apply to city blocks.

As a document of spatial regulations the Ordonnance turns out to be much more effective and much more stringent than edicts dealing with urban public utilities, as had been promulgated since the time of Henri II. Indeed, the only prior examples of spatial regulation concerned urban settings. Most of these texts, beginning with the following declaration of May 14, 1554, are concerned with curtailing projecting elements:

As the late king, our most honored Lord and Father (may God absolve him) had wished and decreed for the decoration and well-being of our good city of Paris, for the health of her inhabitants and to keep the streets as clean, clear, and accessible as possible, the projections of old houses into the road should be within a certain time knocked down and cleared away, and none of the repairing and rebuilding of these houses should be undertaken in the said streets and passages; in the same way we have wished, ordered, and decreed since our succession to the crown.[34]

The famous policy statement of September 22, 1600, which is generally cited as the first establishment of building permits in France, is likewise concerned only with building alignments and corners:

It is forbidden for all masons, carpenters, and other workers to make any buildings, sections of wall, cradle irons (*jambes étrières*), or other constructions on the streets, without having first verified the building-line (*alignement*) from the road inspector (*voyer*) or his assistant; as for the building-lines at the corners of streets, it is hereby decreed that they will be determined by the road inspector or by his assistant in the presence of the civil lieutenant and the Procureur du Roi, as has always been the custom.

An enforcement of December 1607 even allows for inspections to verify that these standards have been met.

Although it goes further with respect to proprietors, the edict of July 1609 fixing the "policy regarding dilapidated buildings and unoccupied or undeveloped plots (*places vides et vagues*)" is really just concerned with empty spaces, in an effort to produce presentable façades:

We in our full power and royal authority have ordered and decreed, [and we] desire, order, and decree, that within six months all persons of whatever standing who lay claim to any space or building in our city and suburb, including ecclesiastics, chapters, religious communities, and guardians of minors, will be held responsible for rebuilding them, at least for the buildings facing onto the streets.[35]

Not until 1641 is there a text concerned with height limitations, prescribing that houses located in the suburbs or near the city gates should not be as tall as those situated within the walls.[36] The *Arrêt du Conseil du Roi* of May 16, 1641 indicates this tendency to manage urban prospects and require all applicants to participate proportionally in road repairs. Indeed, current authorizations for housing developments are modeled on the same principle.

The *arrêt* in question deals with paving the main street of the Faubourg Saint-Antoine.[37] It requires the owners of inherited property adjoining the road to have paved, at their own expense, the stretch of road immediately in front of their façade. Those who do so receive the king's permission "to build houses, provided however that they not erect their buildings more than one story above the ground floor."

If we compare these writings with certain articles of the 1699 Ordonnance des Eaux et Forêts, we see that the latter inaugurate mass regulation of land plots, an entirely new feature. We can therefore conclude that modern documents of building density or land acquisition and restoration (especially floor occupancy plans) are derived from this text. The passage in question reads as follows:

We enjoin all of our subjects, without exception or difference, to regulate the cutting of their brushwood to ten years at minimum, and they will be obliged to reserve ten [trees] for each *arpent*, and they will be obliged also to reserve ten from ordinary sales of full-grown trees, in order, however, to dispose of them for their own profit, after the age of forty years for brushwood and one hundred twenty years for full-grown trees, and moreover they [must] observe in the exploitation of said cutting the regulations governing the use of our woods, on pain of sanctions prescribed in the *ordonnances*.[38]

Colbert's reform is therefore not restricted to royal forests and various surveys. It tends to homogenize the wooded space beyond the right of property, the effects of which it limits by imposing certain thresholds of density based on the age of the trees. And thus we see an entirely new concern for the relation of height to density.

Articles 4 and 16 of Ordonnance XXVII also provide for the making of "maps, figures and descriptions," to be submitted to the clerk's office for every Maîtrise des Eaux et Forêts. The notion of a zone *non aedificandi* also appears: "We forbid all persons to build in the future any châteaux, farms, and houses within the confines of, on the banks of, or within half a league of our forests."[39] Not to mention the concern with establishing traffic signals: "We order that at corners of crossings, where two or three roads intersect along the highways and royal roads of the forests, the officers of the various maîtrises will immediately plant crosses, posts or pyramids, at our expense and with wood belonging to us."[40]

Rather than ascribing a new "forest" metaphor to the city, we should recognize from these excerpts the far-reaching effects of this document. At the very least, we should acknowledge the debt that every urban planner and developer owes, on the level of methodology, to this technique of placing quotas on space—the model for which already exists in Colbert's 1669 Ordonnance.

Conclusion

Development (*aménagement*) on a territorial scale is a forward-looking notion based on long-term economic policy. Its goal is the organization of space, improvement of the environment through physical planning and economic programs. All the efforts of seventeenth-century monarchs and politicians point in this direction. And as we have tried to demonstrate, during this period the garden is at the heart of the debate, whether as a place for technical experimentation, a model of organization, or a counterpart to large-scale projects. This world in which Le Nôtre was born and lived, and which he stamped with his personal contributions, neatly coincides with the emergence in France of a desire for nationwide organization.

Our living space, in its totality, is still conceived along frequently misguided criteria that are an inheritance of the classic age. Our cities, from Versailles to Hausmann's Paris, are still profoundly marked by these conceptions. There is nothing, down to the products of Le Corbusier's Charter of Athens and the now much-derided mega-schemes themselves, that cannot be considered the final avatars of an axial and monumental composition totally perverted by abstract considerations and academicians. Today, impact studies and the work of organizations devoted to protecting the national heritage are forcing us to rediscover the necessity of adapting to the existing site, whose fundamental importance we have seen in the projects of the seventeenth century.

The great lesson of seventeenth-century landscapists, and hence of Le Nôtre, is that we need to relearn how to take advantage of the surroundings while realizing that they cannot be frozen in time. The picturesque trees (lopsided, fallen, covered in mistletoe and ground ivy) that have been the marvel of generations from Jean-Jacques Rousseau to the Romantics to the ecologists are nothing but an image of obsolescence that some would like to preserve at all costs. The protection of sites involves their management first and foremost; landscape makes sense only when considered in terms of movement, the renewal of societies, agrarian forms, and the ways in which we occupy the land. Traditional pictorial conceptions and vegetal conservatism present no long-term solutions. A tamed nature, but one whose fundamental laws are nonetheless respected, is ultimately more attractive and profitable in every respect than the Amazonian nostalgias haunting our culture. The classical heritage does not reside in grand simplifying schemas; rather, it should guide us in a method of management based on a subtle and coherent analysis.

Notes

Chapter 1

1. Hardouin de Beaumont de Péréfixe, *Histoire du Roi Henry le Grand* (Paris: Edmé Martin, 1661), p. 246.

2. Ibid., p. 322.

3. Martine Gorrichon, *Les travaux et les jours à Rome et dans l'ancienne France: les agronomes latins inspirateurs d'Olivier de Serres* (Université de Tours, 1976).

4. Jacques Androuet du Cerceau, *Livre d'architecture auquel sont contenus diverses ordonnances de plans et élévation de bâtiments pour seigneurs, gentilshommes et autres qui voudront bâtir aux champs* (Paris, 1582).

5. The declaration of 31 July 1626 prescribes "that in all *places forts*, whether cities or châteaux, that are in the midst of our kingdom and its provinces, and that are not located in significant places (such as borders or other important areas), the fortifications should be razed or demolished; this includes old and weak walls, as is judged necessary for the good and the calm of our subjects, and the security of this state, in order that henceforth our subjects will not view these places as any kind of inconvenience, and that we will be unburdened of the expense that we are constrained to pay for the garrisons."

6. Jacques Androuet du Cerceau, *Les plus excellents bâtiments de France* (Paris, 1576).

7. Jean-Pierre Babelon, *Demeures parisiennes sous Henri IV et Louis XIII* (Paris: Le Temps, 1964).

8. De Péréfixe, *Histoire du Roi Henry le Grand*, p. 321.

9. Marc Bloch, *Les caractères originaux de l'histoire rurale française* (Paris: Armand Colin), 1932, p. 20.

10. Barthélemy de Laffemas, *Règlement général pour dresser les manufactures en ce royaume* (Paris: Claude de Monstroeil, 1597) Laffemas was appointed to the control of commerce in 1602.

11. Antoine de Montchrétien, *Traité de l'économie politique dédié au roi et à la reine mère du roi en 1615*, critical edition by Th. Funck Brentano (Paris: Plon, 1889).

12. Olivier de Serres, *La théâtre d'agriculture et mesnage des champs* (Paris, A. Saugrain, 1603), book V, ch. XV, "La cueillette de la soie pour la nourriture des vers qui la font," p. 458.

13. Ibid., p. 460.

14. Barthélemy de Laffemas, *Le plaisir de la noblesse et autres des champs sur le profit et preuve certaine du plant des meuriers* (Paris: Pierre Pautonnier, 1603), p. 4.

15. Contract of 23 December 1603 between the Royal Council, Hugues Cosnier, and Jean le Tellier for the development of silkworm breeding in Poitou.

16. Submission by Hugues Cosnier on 11 March 1604 concerning work on the Briare canal. He agrees to complete it within three years and to transplant excess mulberry bushes along the levees.

17. Papers of Sully (Archives Nationales 120 AP 48-1, folios 19 and 24).

18. The term *nationalisme économique* is borrowed from Richard Gascon in Fernand Braudel and Ernest Labrousse, eds., *Histoire économique et sociale de la France*, Part 1, (*1450-1660*), vol. 1, *L'état et la ville* (Pierre Chaunu and Richard Gascon) (Paris: Presses Universitaires de France, 1977), pp. 347ff.

19. Under Colbert one still finds 360 customs or local variants of law.

20. Père Pierre du Val, *Description de la France et de ses provinces* (Paris: Jean Du Puis, 1663, p. 71).

21. André du Chesne, *Les antiquités et recherches des villes, châteaux et places plus remarquables de toute la France* (Paris: J. Petit-Pas, 1609), p. 3.

22. Ibid.

23. Ibid.

24. Père Claude de Varennes, *Le voyage de France dressé pour l'instruction et commodité tant des français que des étrangers* (Paris: O. de Varennes, 1639).

25. (Paris: Th. Le Gras, 1742).

26. Bloch, *Les caractères originaux de l'histoire rurale française*, pp. x, xi.

27. *Histoire économique et sociale de la France*, part 1 (1450-1660), vol. 1 (*l'etat et la ville*), pp. 181ff.

28. Ibid., p. 197.

29. According to Furetière's *Dictionnaire*, suburb (*banlieu*) designates the territory within a league of the city.

30. Michel Mollat, *Histoire de l'Ile-de-France et de Paris* (Toulouse: Privat, 1971), pp. 277ff.

31. On this point see Jean Jacquart, "La production agricole dans la France du XVIIe siècle," *Dix-Septième Siècle* 70-71 (1966): 22-25.

32. *Belles maisons et promenades qui se peuvent faire autour de Paris*. For seventeenth-century châteaux see the special issue of *Dix-Septième Siècle* 118-119 (January-June 1978) edited by Georges Poisson.

33. The Pavé du Roy refers to the Fontainebleau road (now the Nationale 7).

34. Josiane Sartre, *Châteaux "brique et pierre" en France* (Paris: Nouvelles Éditions Latines, 1981).

35. Page xxxv of the volume concerning the estate of Claude Gallard I, preserved in the archives of the Département of Essonne.

Chapter 2

1. Du Chesne, *Les antiquités*, p. 2.

2. Ibid., p. 232.

3. On this point, see Pierre Goubert, "Economie et urbanisme en France dans la première moité du XVIIe siècle," in *L'urbanisme de Paris et de l'Europe 1600-1680* (unpublished works presented by Pierre Francastel), pp. 38ff.

4. Nicolas Delamare, *Traité de la police*, vol. 3 (Paris: Michel Brunet, 1719), p. 338.

5. Ibid., p. 338.

6. Ibid., p. 338.

7. Adolphe Berty, *Topographie historique du vieux Paris*, vol. 2, *Région du Louvre et Tuileries* (Paris: Imprimerie Nationale, 1868), p. 179.

8. Vol. 3, p. 390.

9. Berty, *Topographie du vieux Paris*, p. 204.

10. Ibid., p. 211.

11. Ibid., p. 219.

12. Archives Nationales 01 1046 21.

13. Jacques Boyceau de la Baraudière, *Traité du jardinage selon les raisons de la nature et de l'art* (Paris: M. Van Lochon, 1636).

14. On this point see *Revue du XVIIe Siècle* 9–10 (1951): 533.

15. Boyceau de la Baraudière, *Traité du jardinage*, p. 30.

16. Archives Nationales 01 1045, p. 3. Privileges granted to workers residing in the Louvre gallery.

17. René Crozet, *La vie artistique en France au XVIIe siècle* (Paris: Presses Universitaires de France, 1954), p. 15.

18. Marie-Antoinette Fleury, *Documents du minutier central concernant les peintres, sculpteurs et graveurs au XVIIe siècle* (Paris: Imprimerie Nationales, 1969).

19. Antoine Dézallier d'Argenville, *Abrégé de la vie des plus fameux peintres*, vol. 2 (Paris: De Bure, 1745), p. 240.

20. Fleury, *Documents*, pp. 746–56 (inventory of the property of Simon Vouet, 26 June 1640, on the occasion of his remarriage).

21. Dézallier d'Argenville, *Abrégé*, vol. 2, p. 241.

22. Maurice Daumas, *Les instruments scientifiques aux XVIIe et XVIIIe siècles* (Paris: Presses Universitaires de France, 1953). (Available in English as *Scientific Instruments of the Seventeenth and Eighteenth Centuries*, ed. and trans. Mary Holbrook [New York: Praeger, 1972].)

23. Alkmaar and Berg-op-Zoom.

24. Antoine Dézallier d'Argenville, *La théorie et pratique du jardinage* (Paris: Jean-Pierre Mariette, 1747), p. 105 of chapter 1 of Part II devoted to practical geometry.

25. Pierre Vernier, *La construction, l'usage et les propriétés du quadrant nouveau de mathématiques* (Brussels: F. Vivien, 1631).

26. Philippe Danfrie, *Déclaration de l'usage du graphomètre, par la pratique duquel l'on peut mesurer toutes distances . . . arpentes, terres, bois, prés et faire plans de villes, forteresses, cartes, géographiques* (Paris, 1597).

27. Ibid., p. 7.

28. Jules Guiffrey, *Comptes des bâtiments du roi sous le règne de Louis XIV*, vol. 1 (Paris: Imprimerie Nationale, 1881), p. 1059.

29. Elie Vinet and Antoine Mizauld, *La maison champêtre et agriculture* (Paris: Robert Fouet, 1607).

30. Jean Leclerc, *Théâtre géographique du royaume en France* (Paris: J. Le Clerc, 1620). From Damien de Templeux we possess a *Converture de l'Ile-de-France, du Beauvaisis, de la Champagne, de la Brie et de la Beauce en 1631*. Nicolas Tassin, *Les cartes générales de toutes les provinces de France, royaumes et provinces de l'Europe* (Paris, 1638).

31. Pierre Bourdin, *Le cours de mathématiques dédié à la noblesse*, 3rd ed. (Paris: Simon Bernard, 1661), p. 4.

32. Révérend Père François de Dainville, "L'enseignement des mathématiques au dix-septième siècle," *Dix-Septième Siècle* 30 (1956): 62–68.

33. The notions of command, esplanade, and ridge, proper to fortification, are here applied intentionally.

34. Père Georges Fournier, *Traité des fortifications ou architecture militaire* (Paris: Jean Hénault, 1648), p. 41.

35. Bourdin, *Le cours de mathématiques*, p. 70.

36. Ibid., p. 100.

37. On this point see Emilio Sereni, *Histoire du paysage rural italien*, pp. 47ff. (Original

in Italian; available in English as *History of the Italian agricultural landscape* [Princeton, N.J.: Princeton University Press, 1997].)

38. Le Nôtre's master Simon Vouet was mainly an interior decorator.

39. Roger De Piles, *Abrégé de la vie des peintres avec des réflexions sur leurs ouvrages et un traité du peintre parfait*, ch. XVII, *Du paysage* (Paris: F. Muguet, 1699), p. 47.

40. Ibid., p. 2.

41. Ibid., p. 3.

42. Manuscript M 810, *Dialogue sur le coloris*, p. 4.

43. Louis Savot, *L'architecture française des bâtiments particuliers* (Paris: Jack Villery, 1685), p. 56 (first edition 1632).

44. Du Chesne, *Les antiquités*, p. 2.

45. François Savinien d'Alquie, *Les délices de la France* (Leyden: Théodore Haak, 1728), p. 200.

46. Ibid., p. 201.

47. Sébastien le Prestre de Vauban, *Méthode générale et facile pour faire le dénombrement des peuples* (Paris: A. Chrestien, 1686), p. 5.

48. Père Jean François, *La science de la géographie* (Rennes: J. Hardy, 1652), p. 33.

Chapter 3

1. Guillaume de Lorris and Jean de Meung, *Le roman de la Rose* (Paris: Gallimard, 1949), pp. 21–40.

2. *Le jardin de plaisance et fleur de réthorique*, cited in Frédéric Lachevre, *Bibliographie des recueils collectifs de poésies du XVIᵉ siècle* (Paris: Honoré Champion, 1922), p. 3.

3. Gorrichon, *Les travaux et les jours à Rome et dans l'ancienne France*, p. 11.

4. De Serres, *Le théâtre d'agriculture et mesnage des champs*, p. 456.

5. Boyceau de la Baraudière, *Traité du jardinage*, p. 27.

6. Ibid., ch. XIV, p. 82.

7. Ibid., p. 81.

8. Ibid., p. 69.

9. Ibid., ch. 3, p. 71.

10. Ibid., p. 69.

11. Ibid., ch. 2, p. 70.

12. Ibid., p. 71.

13. Ibid., p. 75.

14. Ibid., p. 75.

15. Ibid., p. 82.

16. Ibid., p. 72.

17. Sieur de Sainctyon, *Les édits et ordonnances des rois, coutumes des provinces, reglements arrêtes et jugements notables des eaux et forêts* (Paris: Langlier, 1610).

18. Du Chesne, *Les antiquités*, p. 375.

19. Ibid., p. 329.

20. De Serres, *Le théâtre d'agriculture et mesnage des champs*, Part 1, ch. 4, p. 16.

21. Pierre Grimal, "Jardins des hommes, jardins des rois" *Traverses*, 5–6 (October 1976): 70.

22. Pierre Grimal, *Les jardins romains* (Paris: Presses Universitaires de France, 1969), p. 315.

23. Etienne Taillemite, "Le problème de la marine de guerre au XVIIᵉ siècle," *Revue du XVIIᵉ Siècle* 86–87 (1970): 21.

24. P. Noisy, "Note sur la galerie des glaces," *Revue du XVIIe Siècle* 53 (1961): 49.

25. Jacques de Gaffarel, *Le monde souterrain* (Paris: Charles du Mesnil, 1654).

26. Louis Hautecoeur, *Histoire de l'architecture classique en France* (Paris: Picard, 1943–57), vol. 1, book 2, *La formation de l'idéal classique*, p. 224.

27. Jacqueline Thuerillat, *Les mystères de Bomarzo et des jardins symboliques de la Renaissance* (Geneva: Les Trois Annexes, 1973), p. 258.

28. The notion of a visual grammar appears in a work by Aloïs Riegl (*Historische Grammatik der bildenden Künste*, ed. Karl M. Swoboda and Otto Pächt [Graz: Bohlau, 1966]).

29. Boyceau de la Baraudière, *Traité du jardinage*, p. 73.

30. Antoine Dézallier d'Argenville, *La théorie et pratique du jardinage*, 4th ed. (Paris: Jean-Pierre Mariette, 1747).

31. The administrative plans are preserved in the Departmental Archives of Les Yvelines.

32. Rosny, the only surviving park in Les Yvelines, is a very typical instance of adaptation to the site.

33. Antoine Dézallier d'Argenville, *Voyage pittoresque des environs de Paris, au descripton des maisons royales, châteaux et autres lieux de plaisance situés à quinze lieues aux environs de cette ville* (Paris: De Bure, 1755), pp. 206–7.

34. Ibid., p. 207.

35. Ibid., p. 347.

36. Ibid., p. 261.

37. Bibliothèque Nationale, Manuscripts, MSS MA Fr 22 936.

38. Louis de Rouvroy, due de Saint-Simon, *Mémoires*, vol. 12, ch. 19, year 1715 (Paris: J. de Bonnot, 1967).

39. Nicodemus Tessin, "Voyage de Versailles en 1687," *Revue de l'Histoire de Versailles et de Seine-et-Oise* (1926): 160.

40. Dézallier d'Argenville, *Voyage*, p. 16.

41. Charles Perrault, *Mémoires* (Avignon, 1759), p. 150.

42. Tessin, "Voyage de Versailles," p. 292.

43. Stockholm, Nationalmuseum, THC 2114–23.

44. Jean Cordey, *Vaux-le-Vicomte* (Paris: Albert Morancé, 1924), p. 94.

45. Boris Losski, *J. B. A. Leblond, architecte de Pierre le Grand* (Prague, 1936).

46. Ibid., p. 187.

47. Dézallier d'Argenville, *La théorie et pratique du jardinage* (Paris: P. J. Mariette, 1747), p. 15.

48. Ibid., ch. 1.

Chapter 4

1. Charles Perrault, *Memoirs of My Life*, ed. and trans. by Jeanne Morgan Zarucchi (Columbia: University of Missouri Press, 1989), p. 41; original French in *Mémoires* (Avignon, 1759), p. 29.

2. Ibid., pp. 107–8 (translation); 186–88 (original French).

3. Pierre Clément, *Lettres, instructions et mémoires de Colbert* (Paris, 1867), p. 368.

4. All this information is taken from Guiffrey's edition of the *Comptes des bâtiments du roi*.

5. Ibid., p. 256.

6. Ibid., p. 257.

7. Ibid., p. 340.

8. Thomas Francini, 1571-1651.

9. "Voyage de Versailles," p. 289.

10. Guiffrey, *Comptes des bâtiments du roi*, p. 482.

11. Ibid., p. 578.

12. Martin Lister, *A Journey to Paris in the Year 1698*, 3rd ed. (London: Jacob Tonson, 1699) (reprinted Urbana: University of Illinois Press, 1967) pp. 38-39.

13. Père Pierre Nicolas Desmolets, *Continuation des mémoires de littérature et d'histoire de Monsieur de Salengre* (Paris: Simart, 1726), p. 464.

14. Ibid., p. 467.

15. Guiffrey, *Comptes des bâtiments du roi*, pp. 47ff.

16. Charles Perrault, *Parallèle des anciens et des modernes* (Paris: J. B. Coignard, 1697), pp. 84-85.

17. Desmolets, *Continuation des mémoires*, p. 464.

18. Guiffrey, *Comptes des bâtiments du roi*, p. 587.

19. Ibid., p. 700.

20. *Histoire de l'Académie royale des sciences*, vol. 1, 1666-86, (Paris: J. B. Coignard, 1733), p. 260.

21. Pierre Le Muet, *Manière de bien bâtir pour toutes sortes de personnes* (Paris, 1623).

22. Jean-Marie Pérouse de Montclos, *L'architecture à la française* (Paris: Picard, 1982), ch. 6, *La distribution intérieure*, p. 60.

23. Boyceau de la Baraudière, *Traité du jardinage*, ch. VI, p. 74.

24. Dézallier d'Argenville, *La théorie et la pratique du jardinage* (4th ed., 1647), ch. IV.

25. Ibid., ch. VI.

26. Ibid., p. 19.

27. *Traité du jardinage*, p. 71.

28. Ibid., p. 73.

29. On this point see Michel Devèze, *La grande réformation des forêts sous Colbert* (Université de Paris, 1954), p. 11.

30. Jousse, Daniel, *Commentaire de l'ordonnance des eaux et forêts du mois de 1669* (Paris: De Bure, 1772), p. 72.

31. Ibid., article 21, p. 75.

32. Ibid., p. 214.

33. Ibid., p. 214.

34. Delamare, *Continuation du traité de la police* (Paris: J. F. Hérissant, 1738), vol. 4, p. 324.

35. Ibid., p. 358.

36. Ibid., p. 394.

37. Ibid., p. 394.

38. Jousse, *Commentaire de l'ordonnance*, title XXXVI, *Des bois appartenant aux particuliers*, article 1, p. 320.

39. Ibid., p. 343.

40. Ibid., p. 365.

Glossary

Below are basic definitions of many of the more important specialized terms found in the text. For fuller definitions of these and other terms, see François Bluche, ed. *Dictionnaire du Grand Siècle* (Paris: Fayard, 1990), Michel Conan, *Dictionnaire historique de l'art des jardins* (Paris: Hazan, 1997), and Sir Geoffrey Jellicoe et al., eds., *The Oxford Companion to Gardens* (Oxford and New York: Oxford University Press, 1986). — G.L.

Allée — A garden walk, generally consisting of packed earth covered in sand or gravel (for walking), or covered in turf and lined with arching trees (for riding).

Aménagement — The French term for planning or development, *aménagement* has more general implications of managing, arranging, subdividing, distributing, ordering, or putting together.

Arpent — Surface measurement equal to 3,418.86 m² (36,800 square feet) in Paris. The *arpent* of the Eaux et Forêts, used by the Ordonnances, measures 5167.2 m² (55,619 square feet).

Arrêt — Legal document communicating decisions of the king and his council.

Bâtiments du roi — At the most basic level, the "king's buildings" comprise royal residences and other royal building projects such as urban renovations. During the sixteenth century the maintenance and care of royal buildings had been entrusted to a *superintendant* or *surintendant* in charge of each project. There was a move toward centralization with the election of Sully to the *surintendance* in 1602, and the post became an office in 1616. At the time the surintendant was assisted by a contrôleur général and two treasurers, who oversaw financial matters. By the time Jean-Baptiste Colbert was elected *Surintendant et ordonnateur général des bâtiments, arts, tapisseries et manufactures de beaux-arts* in 1664, the post had effectively become a Ministry of Arts controlling all aspects of royal buildings, arts, manufactures, and sciences. Its reach extended to such matters as gardens, the royal library and press, academies, and festivals.

Berceau — A vaulted arbor of trellis-work.

Bosquet — An ornamental grove, thicket, or shrubbery pierced by walks.

Boulingrin — An ornamental sunken lawn or turf parterre, corruption of the English words "bowling green."

Broderie — Embroidery. In gardens, designates parterre ornaments generally consisting of low bushes in the form of winding abstract vegetal patterns.

Cabinet (de verdure) — An intimate outdoor room with walls of foliage, open to the sky.

Carré d'eau — A rectangular expanse of water.

Chambre des comptes — Judicial and administrative body in charge of royal finances, titles of nobility, and matters of the royal domain.

Conseiller (du roi)—Designates a royal office on any level. In its strictest sense *conseiller* refers to a magistrate or to a councilor in the Parlement or some other sovereign court.

Contre-allée – Name given to each secondary *allée* flanking a principal one.

Corps de logis—The principal block of a residential building, as distinct from wings or pavilions.

Département—Administrative subdivision in modern France, established at the time of the Revolution.

Droits de justice—Judicial rights in a seigneurie, granted by the king to the seigneur. These range from lesser jurisdiction (*basse justice*) over matters like propery and contracts, to extensive jurisdiction (*haute justice*) including the right to sentence subjects to death.

Eaux et Forêts—During the Ancien Régime the administration of water and forests was overseen by a body of royal officials. These included the Grandes Maîtrises des Eaux et Forêts and, below them, the *maîtrises particulières*. Their control over the forests became increasingly ineffectual over the course of the seventeenth century until Colbert's great reformation of the forest administration, culminating in the with the *Ordonnance des Eaux et Forêts* of August 1669.

Élection—Administrative subdivision under the ancien régime, used for tax collection. See *généralité*.

Espalier—Term (adapted from the Italian *spalliera*) designating a wall or fence along which fruit trees are planted at regular intervals. Since the end of the seventeenth century *espalier* has designated a manner of planting and directing the growth of fruit trees.

Financier—A class of professionals devoted to supplying the money necessary for the functioning of the state, whether by means of public administration of finances or by engaging in private services supporting public finances.

Fleuron—An ornament shaped like a flower or leaf.

Fruictier/fruitier—A garden devoted to the production of fruit trees.

Gazon – A term equivalent to the English "turf," signifying a covering of grass and other plants along with their matted roots.

Généralité—One of the financial districts into which ancien régime France was subdivided for administrative purposes. These included both *pays d'élections*, in which a board of elected officials (*élus*) settled on the amounts to be collected, and the *pays d'états*, in which the provincial estates determined the total. During the seventeenth century, each *généralité* was governed by a *maître des requêtes*. Toward the mid-seventeenth century the latter title was changed to *intendant* (of justice, police, and finance), hence the frequent substitution of the word *intendance* for *généralité*.

Glacis—A gently and evenly sloping terrain, found in fortifications and in gardens where it is generally covered in turf.

Hôtel particulier—A type of French private town house established in the mid-sixteenth century, traditionally consisting of a *corps de logis* placed between a rear garden and a forecourt. The forecourt is generally enclosed by narrow wings extending to a screen wall (or else a stable and kitchen block) with a central portal opening onto the street.

Intendant—The chief provincial royal official, usually assigned to a specific territory.

Livre (tournois)—A basic unit of currency, equal to twenty-two *sous*.

Maître des requêtes—Judiciary officers in charge of a *généralité*.

Maîtrise—See *Eaux et Forêts*.

Orangerie—An enclosed building space used for the conservation of plants that cannot survive the winter outside. Alternatively, a garden adjoining such a building, allowing for the exposure of oranges to sunlight.

Ordonnance—A legislative text passed by the French king. Louis XIV carried out a reformation of the realm with the five *Grands Ordonnances* between 1667 and 1681, including the *Ordonnance des Eaux et Forêts* of 1669. See also *Eaux et Forêts*.

Palissade—In gardens, a screen of trees or shrubs cropped closely to an equal height and width, thus forming a wall.

Parc—Traditionally an area of land set aside for the raising and hunting of game.

Parlement—Although there were numerous provincial Parlements by the seventeenth century, the term generally refers to the highest sovereign court, located in Paris, which was responsible for important legal duties including delivering *arrêts*.

Parterre—A continuous expanse of terrain, generally horizontal, in which the various components form a single space that can be taken in at a glance. These include *parterres de broderie* (see *broderie*), *parterres à l'anglaise* (with designs of cut turf), and *parterres de pièces coupées* (cut-work parterres) in which the design components are flower-beds.

Patte d'oie—("Goosefoot") Numerous straight *allées* or roads fanning out from a single point of convergence.

Pièce d'eau—A large reflecting pool in a garden.

Plate-bande—A long strip of land, uniform in width (generally 1–3 meters/3–10 feet), in which the plantings (flowering plants, ornamental shrubs, cropped trees) produce a decorative effect. Often sloping in the form of a saddle-back, despite the name.

Police—During the Ancien Régime, police were responsible for maintaining public order in urban areas. Their functions were judiciary as well as executive.

Quincunx—A manner of planting trees extending over a large area, with a tree at each corner and at the centre of a series of squares (sixteenth century) and, beginning around the seventeenth century, disposed only in the corners of squares.

Rocaille—Architectural decoration made up of rocks and shells, a technique originating in ancient Rome and revived in Renaissance Europe.

Saut-de-loup—A large ditch around the perimeter of a garden, designed to keep out wolves. A "ha-ha" is a hidden *saut-de-loup*, producing an effect of continuity with the terrain outside the garden until one is close enough to be take aback ("aha!") by the gap.

Secrétaire du roi—Official responsible for signing and overseeing acts passed by one of the many chancelleries in Paris or the provinces. Given the lightness of these duties, the position was basically a sinecure.

Seigneur, Seigneurie—The seigneur, or lord, was the master in feudal land management, a medieval system that survived with modifications in the time of Le Nôtre. Seigneurie can equally designate the manor (the land under the jurisdiction of the seigneur) or lordship (the power and rights of the seigneur over lands and persons).

Toise—A measurement equaling 1.96 m, or approximately 6′ 5″.

Vaux affair—Term referring to the arrest and trial of Nicolas Fouquet, Vicomte de Melun et de Vaux and Marquis de Belle-Isle (1615–80). Under Jules Mazarin he was made Procureur-Général to the Parlement of Paris (1650) and then Surintendant des Finances (1653). Fouquet was ambitious to succeed Mazarin (d. 1661), but his hopes were wrecked when he was arrested at Colbert's instigation on 5 September 1661, not long after a lavish fête at his residence of Vaux-le-Vicomte. After being sentenced three years later, Fouquet spent the rest of his life in the prison of Pignerol.

Bibliography

EARLY WORKS

PRACTICAL GEOMETRY

Topography, Cartography, Astronomy

Académie des Sciences. *Divers ouvrages de mathématiques et de physique par Messieurs de l'Académie royale des sciences.* Paris, 1693.
———. *Mémoires de mathématiques et de physique tirés des registres de l'Académie des sciences.* Paris, 1692–1693.
Bion, Nicolas. *Traité de la construction et des usages des instruments mathématiques.* Paris, 1709.
Cassini, Jean-Dominique. *Eléments de l'astronomie.* Paris, 1684.
———. *Mémoire pour servir à l'histoire des sciences et à celle de l'observatoire royal de Paris,* followed by the autobiography of J. D. Cassini. New ed. Paris, 1810.
———. *Oeuvres diverses.* Paris, 1730.
Danfrie, Philippe. *Déclaration de l'usage du graphomètre, par la pratique duquel l'on peut mesurer toutes distances . . . arpenter terres, bois, prés et faire plans de villes, forteresses, cartes géographiques.* Paris, 1597.
Du Hamel, J. B. *Histoire de l'Académie royale des sciences.* Vol. 1, 1666–1699; vol. 2, 1686–1699; vols. 3–11, *Mémoires de 1666–1699.* Paris, 1733.
Finé, Oronce. *La practique de la géométrie.* Paris, 1586.
Fontenelle, Bernard de. *Histoire du renouvellement de l'Académie royale des sciences en 1699.* Amsterdam, 1709.
La Hire, Philippe de. *Observations astronomiques faites en France les années 1680, 81, 82.* Paris, 1682.
———. *La gnomonique.* Paris: E. Michallet, 1682.
———. *L'Ecole des Arpenteurs où l'on enseigne toutes les pratiques de géométrie qui sont nécessaires à un arpenteur.* On y a ajouté un abrégé du nivellement et les propriétés des eaux et les manières de les jauger. Paris: T. Moette, 1689.
———. *Description et explication des globes qui sont placés dans les pavillons du château de Marly, par ordre de sa majesté.* Paris: L.V. Thibout, 1704.
Le Clerc, Sébastien. *Pratique de la géométrie sur le papier et sur le terrain.* Paris: T. Jolly, 1668.
Perrault, Charles. *Parallèle des anciens et des modernes,* vol. 4, où il est traité de l'astronomie, de la géographie, de la navigation, de la guerre. Paris: J. B. Coignard, 1697.
Picard, Abbé Jean. *Mesure de la terre.* Paris: Imprimerie Royale, 1671.

———. *Traité du nivellement, avec une relation de quelques nivellements fairs par ordre du Roi.* Paris: E. Michallet, 1684.

Snellius, called Snell de Roijen. *Doctrinae triangulorum canonicae libri quator, Lugdoni Batavorum, ex officina.* J. Maire, 1627.

Vernier, Pierre. *La construction, l'usage et les propriétés du quadrant nouveau de mathématiques.* Brussels, F. Vivien, 1631.

Fortifications

Bourdin, Père Pierre. *Le dessin ou la perspective militaire.* Paris: G. Bernard, 1655.

———. *Le cours de mathématiques dédié à la noblesse.* 3rd. ed. Paris: Simon Bernard, 1661.

———. *L'architecture militaire, ou l'art de fortifier les places régulières et irrégulières.* Paris: G. Bernard, 1655.

De Ville, Antoine. *Les fortifications.* Paris: T. Quinet, 1636.

Du Breuil, Père Jean. *L'art universel des fortifications.* Paris: J. du Breuil, 1665.

Errard, Jean. *La fortification démontrée et réduite en art.* Paris: 1622.

Fournier, Père Georges. *Traité des fortifications ou architecture militaire.* Paris: J. Hénault, 1648.

François, Père Jean. *L'arithmétique et la géométrie pratique.* Paris: N. Langlois, 1681.

Fritach, Adam. *L'architecture militaire ou la fortification nouvelle.* Leiden: Les Elzéviers, 1635.

Pontault de Beaulieu, Sébastien de. *Plans, profiles et vues de camps, places, sièges, batailles, servant à l'histoire de Louis XIV, classés chronologiquement de 1643 à 1697.* s.l., n.d.

Vauban, Sebastien le Prestre de. *De l'attaque et de la défense des places.* The Hague: P. de Hondt, 1737–1742.

———. *Mémoire pour servir d'instruction dans la conduite des sièges et la défense des places.* Leiden: J. and H. Verbeck, 1740.

GEOGRAPHY, COSMOGRAPHY

Aristotle. *Météorologica.* French translation by J. Barthélémy St-Hilaire. Paris: Ladrange, 1863.

Baudrand, Michel-Antoine. *Lexicon géographicum.* Paris: F. Muguet, 1670. *Dictionnaire géographique et historique* by M. A. Baudrand, ed. Louis Baudrand. Paris: I. de Bats, 1705.

De Renty, Gaston. *Le cosmographe ou introduction facile à la cosmographie.* Paris: F. Clousier, 1645.

Du Val, Pierre. *La connaissance et l'usage des globes et des cartes de géographie.* Paris: L'auteur, 1654.

———. *Alphabet et définition des termes dont on se sert en géographie.* Paris: L'auteur, 1677.

———. *Introduction à la géographie.* Paris: L'auteur, 1679.

Finé, Oronce. *Le sphère du monde proprement dite cosmographique.* Paris: Imprimerie de M. de Vascosan, 1551.

François, Père Jean. *La science de la géographie.* Rennes: J. Hardy, 1652.

Labbé, Père Philippe. *La géographie royale.* Paris: M. Hénault, 1646.

Lenglet-Dufresnoy, Abbé N. *Méthode pour étudier la géographie.* Paris: C. E. Hochereau, 1716.

Pajot, Père Charles. *Despauterius Novus, Flexiae, apud.* Paris: G. Griveau, 1650.

Sanson, Guillaume. *Tables de la géographie ancienne et nouvelle ou méthode pour s'instruire avec facilité de la géographie.* Paris: P. Mariette, 1667.

———. *Introduction à la géographie.* Paris: L'auteur, 1681.

Varenius, called Bernhard. *Géographia generalis.* Amsterdam, 1650. *Géographie générale.* Paris: 1755.

PLANNING, DEVELOPMENT, MANAGEMENT

Waters and Forests

Chauffourt, Jacques de. *Instruction sur le fait des eaux et forêts.* Paris: Janet et Métayer, 1603.
De Gallon. *Conférence de l'ordonnance de Louis XIV du mois d'août 1669, sur le fait des eaux et forêts, avec celles des rois prédécesseurs.* Paris: G. Saugrain, 1725.
Jousse, Daniel. *Commentaire sur l'ordonnance des eaux et forêts du mois d'août 1669.* Paris: Debure, 1772.
Sainctyon, Louis de. *Les édits et ordonnances des rois, coutumes des provinces, reglements ar-rêtes et jugements notables des eaux et forêts.* Paris: Laugelier, 1610.

Hydrography, Hydraulics

Cassan. *La nymphe de Chanceaux ou l'arrivée de la Seine au Château de Marly.* Paris: A. Chré-tien, 1699.
Coulon, Louis. *Les rivières de France ou description géographique et historique du cours et débordement des fleuves, rivières, fontaines, lacs et étangs qui arrosent les provinces du royaume.* Paris: F. Clousier, 1644.
De Caus, Isaac. *Nouvelle invention de lever l'eau plus haut que sa source avec quelques ma-chines mouvantes, par le moyen de l'eau, et un discours de la conduite d'icelle.* London, 1644.
De Caus, Salomon. *Les raisons des forces mouvantes avec diverses machines tant utiles que plaisantes auxquelles sont adjoints plusieurs dessins de grottes et fontaines.* Frankfurt: J. Norton, 1615.
Félibien, André. *Description de la grotte de Versailles.* S. Mabre-Cramoisy, 1672.
Fournier, Père Georges. *Hydrographie, contenant la theorie et la pratique de toutes les parties de la navigation.* Paris: Chez Iean de Paris, 1667.
François, Père Jean. *La science des eaux.* Rennes: P. Hallaudays, 1653.
————. *L'art des fontaines avec l'art de niveler.* Rennes: P. Hallaudays, 1665.
Gaffarel, Jacques de. *Le monde souterrain.* Paris: C. Du Mesnil, 1654.
Harcouet de Longeville. *Description des grandes cascades de la Maison Royale de St-Cloud.* Paris: Vangon, 1706.
Kircher, Père Athanase (Athanasius Kircher). *Mundus subterraneus.* Amsterdam, 1665.
La Mothe le Vayer, François de. *L'hexaméron rustique.* Paris: T. Jolly, 1670.
Lescuyer de la Jonchere, Etienne. *Dissertations sur la machine de Marly, sur les pompes du pont Notre-Dame et de la Samaritaine, avec des remarques très curieuses sur l'hydrau-lique, la mechanique et la fortification.* Paris: F. Delalne, 1718.
Mariotte, Edme. *Traité du mouvement des eaux.* Paris: E. Michallet, 1686.
Masson, Jean Papire. *Descriptio fluminum galliae qua Francis est.* Paris: Quesnel, 1618.
Palissy, Bernard. *Discours admirables de la nature des eaux et fontaines.* Paris: M. Le Jeune, 1580.
Perrault, Pierre. *De l'origine des fontaines.* Paris: P. Le Petit, 1674.
Toricelli, Evangéliste. *Traité de la mesure des eaux courantes de Benoît Castelli, avec un dis-cours de la jonction des mers adressé à Messieurs les Commissaires députés par sa Majesté.* Castres: Imprimerie de B. Bacouda, 1664.

Descriptions of the Kingdom

Alquié, François Savinien d'. *Les délices de la France, ou description des provinces, villes principales, maisons royales, châteaux et autres lieux remarquables de ce beau royaume.* Leiden: T. Haak, 1728.

Boisseau, Jean. *Tableau portatif des Gaules.* Paris: Boisseau, 1646.

Des Rues, François. *Description contenant toutes les singularités des plus célèbres villes et places remarquables du royaume de France.* Rouen: D. Geoffroy, n.d.

Du Chesne, André. *Les antiquités et recherches des villes, châteaux et places plus remarquables de toute la France.* Paris: J. Petit-Pas, 1609.

———. *Dessein de la description entière et accomplie du très florissant et très célèbre royaume de France.* Paris, 1614.

Du Val, Pierre. *Description de la France et de ses provinces.* Paris: J. du Puis, 1663.

Jaillot, Alexis Hubert. *Atlas françois.* Paris: Chez le Sr. Jaillot, 1695.

Leclerc, Jean. *Théâtre géographique du Royaume de France.* Paris: J. Le Clerc, 1620.

Manesson-Mallet, Alain. *Description de l'univers contenant les différents systèmes du monde, les cartes de la géographie ancienne et moderne, les plans et les profils des principales villes.* Paris: D. Thierry, 1683.

Montchretien, Antoine de. *Traité de l'économie politique dédié au roi et à la Reine Mère du Roi en 1615.* Critical edition Th. Funck-Brentano. Paris: Plon, 1889.

Nolin, Jean-Baptiste. *Description du royaume de France contenant ses principales divisions géographiques.* Paris: R. Pepie, 1693.

Piganiol de la Force, Jean-Aymar. *Nouvelle description de la France dans laquelle on voit le gouvernement général de ce royaume, celui de chaque province en particulier et la description des villes, maisons royales, châteaux et monuments les plus remarquables.* Vol. 1, containing the description of the government of the Ile-de-France. s.l., n.d.

Saint-Maurice, Alcide de Bonne case, Sieur de. *Tableau des provinces de France.* Paris: J. B. Loyson, 1644.

———. *Le guide fidèle des étrangers dans le royaume de France contenant la description de toutes les villes, châteaux, maisons de plaisance et autres lieux remarquables.* Paris: E. Loyson, 1672.

Sanson, Nicolas. *Description de la France.* Paris: M. Tavernier, 1639.

Savinier d'Alynes (François-Savinien d'Alquié). *Les délices de la France, ou description des provinces, villes capitales, châteaux et maisons royales.* Amsterdam: P. Mortier, 1699.

Tassin, Christophe. *Les plans et profils de toutes les principales villes et lieux considérables de France.* Paris: Michel Van Lochum, 1636.

———. *Carte générale et particulière de toutes les provinces de France.* 1637.

Varennes, Père Claude de. *Le voyage de France dressé pour l'instruction et la commodité tant des français et des étrangers.* Paris: O. de Varennes, 1639.

Vauban, Sebastian le Prestre de. *Méthode générale et facile pour faire le dénombrement des peuples.* Paris: Chrestien, 1686.

GARDENS

Theory

Beroalde de Verville, François Brouart. *Le tableau des riches inventions du songe de Poliphile.* Paris: Matthieu Guillemot, 1600.

Boyceau de la Baraudière, Jacques. *Traité du jardinage selon les raisons de la nature et de l'Art*, Paris: Van Lochom, 1636.

De La Quintinie, Jean. *Instructions pour les jardins fruitiers et potagers*. s.l., n.d.

De Serres, Olivier. *Le théâtre d'agriculture et mesnage des champs*. Paris: A. Saugrain, 1603.

Dézallier d'Argenville, Antoine-Josephe. *La théorie et la pratique du jardinage*. Paris: Pierre-Jean Mariette, 1747.

Estienne, Charles and Iean Liebault. *L'agriculture et maison rustique*. Lyon: Pierre Rigaud, 1622.

Liger, Louis. *La nouvelle maison rustique*. Paris, 1700.

Mizauld, Antoine and Elis Vinet. *La maison champêtre et agriculture*. Paris: Robert Fouêt, 1607.

Mollet, André. *Le jardin de plaisir*. Stockholm: Henry Kayser, 1651.

Mollet, Claude. *Théâtre des plans et jardinages*. Paris: Charles de Sercy, 1652.

Palissy, Bernard. *Recepte véritable*, Paris: J. J. Dubochet, 1844.

Perrault, Charles. *A Monsieur de la Quintinie, sur son livre de l'instruction des jardins fruitiers et potagers*. 1690.

Pitton de Tournefort, Joseph. *Elémens de botanique*. Paris, 1694.

Rapin, Père René. *Hortorum libri IV, Cum disputatione de cultura hortensi*. Paris, 1665. Translated by Voyron et Gabiot, Paris: Cailleau, 1782.

Descriptions

Dan, le Père. *Trésor des merveilles de Fontainebleau*. Paris, 1642.

De Fer, Nicolas. *Relation de ce qui s'est passé de plus remarquable à Fontainebleau, et qui explique aussi dans quel temps et sous quel règne chaque bâtiment a été fait*. s.l., n.d.

Dézallier d'Argenville, Antoine-Josephe. *Voyage pittoresque des environs de Paris: ou descripton des maisons royales, châteaux et autres lieux de plaisance situés à quinze lieues aux environs de cette ville*. Paris: De Bure, 1755.

Dufresny, Charles. *Entretiens ou amusements sérieux et comiques*. Paris: C. Barbin, 1699.

Félibien, André. *Description du château de Versailles*. Paris: D. Mariette, 1696.

Guilbert, Abbé Pierre. *Description historique des châteaux, bourg et forêts de Fontainebleau*. Paris: A. Cailleau, 1731.

La Fontaine, Jean de. "Le songe de Vaux." In *Contes*. Paris: Jean de Bonnot, 1969.

Le Rouge, Georges-Louis. *Les curiosités de Paris, de Versailles, de Marly, de Vincennes, de St-Cloud et des environs*. Paris: Saugrain, 1716.

Mérigot, J. *Promenade ou itinéraire des jardins de Chantilly*. Paris: Desenne, 1791.

Montpensier, Anne-Marie-Louise d'Orléans. *Mémoires de Mlle. de Montpensier*. Amsterdam: J. Wetstein, 1735.

Morellet, Laurent. *Explication historique de ce qu'il y a de plus remarquable dans la maison royale de Versailles, et en celle de Monsieur à St-Cloud*. Paris: B. C. Nego, 1681.

Piganiol de la Force, Jean-Aymar. *Nouvelle description des châteaux et parcs de Versailles et de Marly*. Paris: Delaulne, 1701.

———. *Description de Paris, de Versailles, de Meudon, de Saint-Cloud, de Fontainebleau et de toutes les autres belles maisons et châteaux des environs de Paris*: Paris: Th. Le Gras, 1742.

Scudéry, Madeleine de. *La promenade de Versailles*. Paris: C. Bardin, 1669.

Tessin, Nicodème. *Relation de sa visite à Marly, Versailles, Clagny, Rueil, St Cloud en 1687*. Versailles: M. Mercier, 1927.

On Le Nôtre

Brice, Germain. *Description nouvelle de ce qu'il y a de plus remarquable dans la ville de Paris.* Paris: N. Le Gras, 1684.

Desmolets, Père Pierre Nicolas. *Continuation des mémoires de littérature et d'histoire de Monsieur de Salengre.* Vol. l, ch. IX. Eulogy of Le Nôtre by his nephew Claude Desgots. Paris: simart 1726.

Lefevre, Antoine-Martial. *Les muses en France ou histoire chronologique de l'origine, du progrès et de l'établissement des belles lettres, des sciences et des beaux-arts dans la France.* Paris: Quillau, 1750.

Lister, Martin. *A Journey to Paris in the Year 1698.* London: Jacob Tonson, 1699.

Nicéron, Père Jean-Pierre. *Mémoires pour servir à l'histoire des hommes illustres dans la république des lettres.* Paris: Briasson, 1727–1745.

Perrault, Charles. *Des hommes illustres qui ont paru en France pendant ce siècles, avec leurs portraits au naturel.* Paris: A. Dezallier, 1696–1700.

Petitot (Claude Bernard). *Collection des mémoires relatifs à l'histoire de France depuis Henri IV jusqu'en 1763.* (table in vol. 78). Paris: Foucault, 1820–1829.

Saint-Simon, Louis de Rouvroy, duc de. *Mémoires.* Paris: J. de Bonnot, 1967.

ARCHITECTURE, PAINTING, PERSPECTIVE

Blondel, François. *Cours d'architecture enseigné à l'Académie royale d'architecture.* Amsterdam: Pierre Mortier, 1698.

Bosse, Abraham. *Manière universelle de Monsieur Desargues pour pratiquer la perspective.* Paris: P. des Hayes, 1648.

———. *Traité des pratiques géométrales et perspectives enseignées dans l'Académie royale de peinture et sculpture.* Paris: A. Bosse, 1665.

———. *Le peintre converti aux précises et universelles règles de son art.* Paris: A. Bosse, 1667.

De Caus, Salomon. *La perspective avec la raison des ombres et lumières.* London: Norton, 1612.

———. *La pratique et démonstration des horloges solaires, avec un discours sur les proportions.* Paris: Hyerosme Drouart, 1624.

Dézallier d'Argenville, Antoine-Josephe. *Abrégé de la vie des plus fameux peintres.* Paris: De Bove, 1745–1752.

Félibien, André. *Fête de Versailles en 1668.* s.l., n.d.

———. *Les divertissements de Versailles donnés par le roi en 1674.* Paris: Jean-Baptiste Coignard, 1674.

———. *Des principes de l'architecture, de la sculpture, de la peinture et des autres arts qui en dependent, avec un dictionnaire des termes propres à chacun de ces arts.* Paris: Jean-Baptiste Coignard, 1676.

———. *Conférences de l'Académie royale de peinture et sculpture.* Amsterdam: E. Roger, 1706.

Fréart, Roland, sieur de Chambray. *Idée de la perfection de la peinture.* Le Mans: Ysambart, 1662.

Jousse, Mathurin. *Le secret d'architecture découvrant fidèlement les traits géométriques, coupes et dérobements nécessaires dans les bâtiments.* La Flèche: Chez Georges Griueau, 1642.

Le Brun, Charles. *Conférence de Monsieur Le Brun sur l'expression générale et particulière.* Paris: E. Picart, 1698.

Nicéron, Père Jean-François. *La perspective curieuse, ou magie artificielle des effets merveilleux.* Paris: Pierre Billaine, 1638.

Piles, Roger de. *Abrégé de la vie des peintres avec des réflexions sur leurs ouvrages et un traité du peintre parfait.* Paris: F. Muguet, 1699.

————. *Dialogue sur le coloris.* Paris: N. Langlois, 1673.

Ripa, César. *Iconologie.* Paris: Mathieu Guillemot, 1644.

Savot, Louis. *L'architecture française des bâtiments particuliers.* Paris: Jacques Villery, 1685 (first ed. 1632).

PHILOSOPHY

Descartes, René. *Discours de la méthode, plus la dioptrique, les météores, la méchanique et la musique qui sont des essais de cette méthode.* Paris: Charles Angot, 1668.

————. *Les principes de la philosophie.* Paris: Nicolas Le Gras, 1659.

————. *Le monde.* Paris: Nicolas Le Gras, 1664.

Faret, Nicolas. *L'honnête homme ou l'art de plaire à la cour.* Paris: T. du Bray, 1630.

Mersenne, Père Marin. *Les méchaniques de Galilée.* Paris: H. Guénon, 1634.

Pascal, Blaise. *De l'esprit géométrique.* Paris: F. Alcan, 1886.

NEWSPAPERS

Le Journal des Savants, from 1667.

Le Mercure Galant, from 1672.

WORKS OF THE NINETEENTH AND TWENTIETH CENTURIES

PLANNING, DEVELOPMENT, MANAGEMENT

Waters and Forests

Baluffe, A. *Etudes d'histoire locale: Pierre-Paul Riquet.* Béziers, 1880.

Barbet, L. A. *Les grandes eaux de Versailles.* Paris: Dunod et Pinat, 1907.

Batiffol, Louis. *Notes sur Soualem Rennequin, constructeur de la machine de Marly.* Versailles: Decerf, s.d.

Bondois, Paul. *Deux ingénieurs au siècle de Louis XIV, Vauban et Riquet.* Paris, 1886.

Caron, Abbé J. J. *Notice sur l'ancienne machine de Marly.* Versailles: Montalant-Bougleux, s.d.

Decampe, L. A. *Eloge de Pierre-Paul Riquet.* Paris, 1812.

Des Devises du Dezert, T. A. *Pierre-Paul Riquet, histoire d'une idée, 1650–1681,* Caen, 1881.

Devèze, Michel. *La vie de la forêt française au XVIe siècle.* Paris: Imprimerie Nationale, 1961.

————. *La grande réformation des forêts sous Colbert.* Nancy: 9 Thomas, 1962.

Gondouin, A. M. *Sur la machine de Marly,* Paris: L'auteur, 1803.

Mousset, Albert. *Les Francine: créateurs des eaux de Versailles, intendants des eaux et fontaines de France de 1623 à 1784.* Paris: H. de Champion, 1930.

Riquet de Bon Repos, Pierre-Paul. *Histoire du canal de Languedoc, rédigée sur les pièces authentiques conservées à la bibliothèque impériale et aux archives du canal, par ses descendants.* Paris: Deterville, 1805.

Geography, Cartography, Fortifications

Bonnardot, Alfred. *Paris au XVIIe siècle: Notice sur le plan de Mathieu Mérian.* Paris: n.d.
Chotard, Henry. *Louis XIV, Louvois, Vauban et les fortifications du Nord de la France d'après les lettres inédites de Louvois.* Paris: Plon, 1889.
Dainville, Père François de. *La géographie des humanistes.* Paris: Beauchesne, 1940.
———. *L'enseignement de l'histoire et de la géographie et le ratio studiorum.* Rome, 1954.
———. *Le langage des géographes.* Paris: Picard, 1964.
De Bus, Charles. *Gaston d'Orléans et ses collections topographiques.* Paris: Imprimerie Nationale, 1941.
Faille, René. *Vauban et Cambrai.* s.l., n.d.
Libault, André. *Histoire de la cartographie.* Paris: Chaix.
Parent, Michel. *Vauban.* Paris: Fréal, 1971.
Rebelliau, Alfred. *Vauban.* Paris: Club des Libraires de France, 1962.

ECONOMIC AND SOCIAL HISTORY

Braudel, Fernand. *Ecrits sur l'histoire.* Paris: Flammarion, 1969.
Braudel, Fernand and Etienne Larousse, general eds. *Histoire économique et sociale de la France.* Part 1 (1450–1660), vol. 1, *L'état et la ville.* Paris: Presses Universitaires de France, 1977–82.
Brunet, Pierre. *Structure agraire et économie rurale des plateaux tertiaires entre la Seine et l'Oise.* Caen: Caron, 1960.
Cavaillès, Henri. *La route française, son histoire, sa fonction.* Paris: Armand Colin, 1946.
Chaunu, Pierre. *Economie atlantique, économie mondiale, 1504–1650.* Paris: Méridiens, 1953.
———. *Autour de 1640, politiques et économies atlantiques.* Paris: A. Colin, 1954.
———. *Le bâtiment, enquête d'histoire économique (14e–19e siècles).* Paris: Mouton, 1971.
Clément, Pierre. *Histoire de la vie et de l'administration de Colbert.* Paris: Guillaumin, 1846.
———. *Le gouvernement de Louis XIV.* Paris: Guillaumin, 1848.
Crozet, René. *La vie artistique en France au XVIIe siècle.* Paris: Presses Universitaires de France, 1954.
Duby, Georges and Armand Wallon. *Histoire de la France rurale.* Paris: Seuil, 1975.
Fagniez, Gustave. *L'économie sociale de la France sous Henri IV.* Paris: Hachette, 1897.
Fontenax, M. *Paysans et marchands de l'Essonne.* Paris: Klincksieck, 1957.
Goubert, Pierre. *Cent mille provinciaux au XVIIe siècle.* Paris: Flammarion, 1968.
———. *L'ancien régime.* Paris: A. Colin, 1969.
Jacquart, Jean. *Morangis aux XVIe et XVIIe siècles.* Paris: Klincksieck, 1956.
Mollat, Michel. *Histoire de l'Ile-de-France et de Paris,* sous la direction de M. Mollat. Toulouse: Privat, 1971.
Porchnev, Boris. *Les soulèvements populaires en France au XVIIe siècle.* Paris: Flammarion, 1972.
Rupin, Charles. *Les idées économiques de Sully et leurs applications à l'agriculture, aux finances et à l'industrie.* Rennes: Imprimerie Bretonne, 1907.
Vignon, Eugène. *Etudes historiques sur l'administration des voies publiques en France aux XVIIe et XVIIIe siècles.* Paris: Dunod, 1862.

GARDENS

History

Benoist-Mechin, Jacques. *L'homme et ses jardins*. Paris: Albin Michel, 1975.
Charageat, Marguerite. *L'art des jardins*. Paris: Presses Universitaires de France, 1962.
Gorrichon, Martine. *Les travaux et les jours à Rome et dans l'ancienne France: les agronomes latins inspirateurs d'Olivier de Serres*. Université de Tours, 1976.
Grimal, Pierre. *L'art des jardins*. Paris: Presses Universitaires de France, 1954.
———. *Les jardins romains*. Paris: Presses Universitaires de France, 1969.
Gromort, Georges. *L'art des jardins*. Paris: Vincent-Fréal, 1953.
Hadfield, Miles. *Les jardins*. Paris: Hachette, 1964.
Hautecoeur, Louis. *Les jardins des dieux et des homme*. Paris: Hachette, 1959.
Hazlehurst, Franklin Hamilton. *Jacques Boyceau and the French Formal Garden*. Athens: University of Georgia Press, 1966.
Janne, Françoise. *Bibliographie de l'art et de la théorie des jardins d'agrément de la Renaissance au Romantisme*. Liège, 1966.
Jardins, 1760–1820: pays d'illusion, terre d'expériences. Paris: C.N.M.H., 1977.
Kretzulesco-Quaranta, Emanuela, *Les jardins du songe: "Polyphile" et la mystique de la Renaissance*. Paris: Les Belles Lettres, 1976.
Lequenne, Fernand. *La vie d'Olivier de Serres*. Paris: Julliard, 1970.
Marie, Alfred. *Les jardins français classiques des XVIIᵉ et XVIIIᵉ siècles*. Paris: Vincent Fréal, 1949.
Theurillat, Jacqueline. *Les mystères de Bomarzo et des jardins symboliques de la Renaissance*. Geneva: Les Trois Anneaux, 1973.

Le Nôtre and His Entourage

Babelon, Jean-Pierre. *L'Eglise Saint-Roch à Paris*. Paris: J. Lanore, 1972.
Charageat, Marguerite. *André Le Nôtre et ses dessins*. s.l., n.d.
Corpechot, Lucien. *Les jardins de l'intelligence*. Paris: Emile Paul, 1912.
De Ganay, Ernest. *André Le Nôtre, 1613–1700*. Paris: Vincent Fréal, 1962.
De Mouceaux, Louis. *Notice sur Jean de la Quintinie*. Versailles: Imprimerie de Beau, 1872.
Devilliers, Pierre, *Les leçons du jardin français*. Paris: Société Française des Architectes de Jardins, 1959.
Gabillot, C. *Pièces inédites concernant André Le Nôtre*. Versailles: Librairie Bernard et Dubois, 1912.
Gresy, E. *Documents sur les artistes qui ont travaillé au Château de Vaux, d'après les registres de la paroisse de Maincy*. Paris: Archives de l'Art Français, 1860.
Guiffrey, Jules. *André Le Nostre, étude critique*. Paris: H. Laurens, 1912.
———. *Artistes parisiens du XVIᵉ et du XVIIᵉ siècles, donations, contrats, tirés des insinuations du Châtelet*. Paris: Imprimerie Nationale, 1915.
Lhuillier, Théophile. *Les anciens registres paroissiaux de Maincy*. Meaux, J. Carro, 1870.
Lossky, Boris. *Leblond, architecte de Pierre le Grand*. Prague, 1936.

Site Monographs

Biver, Comte Paul. *Histoire du château de Meudon*. Paris: Jouve, 1923.
Cordey, Jean. *Vaux-le-Vicomte*. Paris: Albert Movancé, 1924.
De Broglie, Raoul. *Chantilly*. Paris: Calmann-Lévy, 1964.

De Nolhac, Pierre. *Histoire du Château de Versailles*. Paris: Société d'Editions Artistiques, 1900.

———. *La création de Versailles*. Versailles: L. Bernard, 1901.

———. *Les bibliothèques du Château de Versailles*. Paris, 1906.

———. *Les jardins de Versailles*. Paris: Goupil, 1906.

De Tanlay, Marguerite. *Le Château de Tanlay*. La Pierre qui Vire, s.d.

Esquiros, Alphonse. *Le Château d'Issy*. Brussels, Taride, 1854.

Giradet, Raoul. *Manière de montrer les jardins de Versailles par Louis SIV*. Paris: Plon, 1951.

Grouchy, Vicomte Emmanuel de. *Meudon, Bellevue et Chaville*. Paris: Société de l'Histoire de Paris, 1893.

Houdard, Georges. *Les châteaux de St-Germain-en-Laye*. s.l., n.d.

Jallut, Marguerite. *Les jardins de Versailles*. Paris: Vincent Fréal, 1948.

Macon, Gustave. *Les arts dans la maison de Condé*. Paris: Libraire d'Art Ancien et Modern, 1903.

Magne, Emile. *Le Château de St-Cloud*. Paris: Calmann-Lévy, 1932.

Mellerio, A., *Marly-le-Roi*. Marly: L. Desveaud, 1926.

Perate, André. *Le parterre d'eau du parc de Versailles sous Louis XIV*. Versailles: L. Bernard, 1899.

ART HISTORY AND AESTHETICS

Babelon, Jean-Pierre. *Demeures parisiennes sous Henri IV et Louis XIII*. Paris: Le Temps, 1964.

Baltrusaïtis, Jurgis. *Aberrations*. Paris: O. Perrin, 1957.

———. *Anamorphoses*. Paris: O. Perrin, 1969.

Braham, Allan and Peter Smith. *François Mansart*. London, A. Zwemmer, 1973.

Caillois, Roger. *Cohérences aventureuses*. Paris: Gallimard, 1976.

Charpentrat, Pierre. *L'art baroque*. Paris: Presses Universitaires de France, 1967.

Deierkauf-Holsboer, S. Wilma. *Histoire de la mise en scène de 1600 à 1673*. Paris: Nizet, 1960.

Dumur, Guy. *Histoire des spectacles*. Paris: Gallimard, 1965.

Dussieux, L. *Mémoires inédits sur la vie et les ouvrages des membres de l'Académie royale de peinture et sculpture*. Paris: Dumoulin, 1854.

Fichet, Françoise. *La théorie architecturale à l'âge classique*. Liège: Mardaga, 1979.

Francastel, Pierre. *La réalité figurative*. Paris: Gonthier, 1965.

———. *Etudes de sociologie de l'art*. Paris: Denoël-Gonthier, 1970.

Guiffrey, Jules. *Les manufactures parisiennes de tapisseries au XVIIe siècle, Nogent-le-Rotrou, Gouverneur*, 1892. Paris: Picard, 1966.

Panofsky, Erwin. *L'oeuvre d'art et ses significations*. Paris: Gallimard, 1969.

———. *Perspective as Symbolic Form*. Trans. Christopher S. Wood. New York: Zone Books, 1991.

Riegl, Aloïs. *Historische Grammatik der bildenden Künste*, ed. Karl M. Swoboda and Otto Pächt. Graz: Bohlau, 1966. French translation *Grammaire historique des arts plastiques*. Paris: Klincksieck, 1978.

Roche, Serge. *Miroirs, galeries et cabinets de glace*. Paris: Hartmann, 1956.

Sociologie de l'art, Francastel et après. Various authors. Paris: Denoël-Gonthier, 1976.

Venturi, Lionello. *Histoire de la critique d'art*. Paris: Flammarion, 1969.

HISTORY OF IDEAS AND OF SCIENCE

Chaunu, Pierre. *A propos du tourant des années 1630–1650*. Caen: L'auteur, 1968.

————. *Aux origines de l'esprit scientifique françis: le XVIIᵉ siècle*. Bar-le-Duc: Imprimerie St-Paul, 1970.

Daumas, Maurice. *Histoire de la science*. Paris: Gallimard, 1957.

————. *Histoire des techniques*. Paris: Presses Universitaires de France, 1965.

Foucault, Michel. *Les mots et les choses*. Paris: Gallimard, 1966.

Koyré, Alexandre. *Etudes galiléennes*. Paris: Hermann, 1939.

————. *Du monde clos à l'univers infini*. Paris: Gallimard, 1973.

Lenoble, Père Robert. *Mersenne ou la naissance du mécanisme*. Paris: Vrin, 1942.

————. *Histoire de l'idée de nature*. Paris: Albin Michel, 1969.

Mandrou, Robert. *Des humanistes aux hommes de sciences*. Paris: Seuil, 1973.

Mornet, Daniel. *Les sciences de la nature au XVIIᵉ siècle*. Paris: Colin, 1911.

Ronchi, Vasco. *Histoire de la lumière*. Paris: A. Colin, 1956.

Rousset, Jean. *L'intérieur et l'extérieur, essais sur la poésie et le théâtre au XVIIᵉ siècle*. Paris: I. Corti, 1968.

Russo, François. *Eléments de bibliographie de l'histoire des sciences et des techniques*. Paris: Hermann, 1969.

Serres, Michel. *Hermès*. Vol. 1, *La communication*; vol. 2, *L'interférence*; vol. 3, *La traduction*. Paris: Minuit, 1968, 1972, 1974.

Taton, René. *Histoire générale des sciences*. Vol. 2, *La science moderne*. Paris: Presses Universitaires de France, 1969.

PERIODICALS

Cahiers de l'Association Internationale des Etudes Françaises 6 (1954): "Le sentiment de la nature au XVIIᵉ siècle."

Dix-Septième Siècle (Bulletin de la Société d'Etude du XVIIᵉ Siècle, 1949–1980).

Gazette Illustrée des Amateurs de Jardins. Since 1913.

Recherches sur le XVIIᵉ Siècle. Annual publication of the Centre d'Histoire des Sciences et des Doctrines. Editions du C.N.R.S. Since 1976.

Revue Henri IV. Appeared from July 1905 to August 1909.

Revue de l'Histoire de Versailles et de Seine-et-Oise. Appeared until 1937.

Index

Translator's Acknowledgments

I would like to thank Series editor John Dixon Hunt and Press editor Jo Joslyn; I am also grateful to Mirka Beneš, David Buisseret, Joseph Leo Koerner, Ingrid Larkin, and Henri Zerner for their enthusiastic support at various stages of the project. Finally, a special thanks to Mark Polizzotti and Tom Conley for their expert editing, and to the Graham Foundation for its generous funding of the translation and the series as a whole.

LaVergne, TN USA
12 September 2010
196636LV00003B/15/P